Medium

How I Learned To Accept My Psychic Abilities

By

Kathy S. DeMatteis

Licensed Massage Therapist, Esthetician, Psychic Medium, Reiki Master, Creator of Foobella's Skin Care, Life Coach

Copyright © 2024 by – Kathy S. DeMatteis – All Rights Reserved.

It is not legal to reproduce, duplicate, or transmit any part of this document in either electronic means or printed format. Recording of this publication is strictly prohibited.

Table of Contents

Author's Thoughts 1
Foreword 9
Spellbound 15
Acknowledgments 17
About The Author 21
Foot Prints 23
Going Back Home 31
Laying on of Hands 37
Not What We've Been Told 43
This Is the House That Love Built 49
Superman 59
My New Reality 65
Transitions 75
Dealing With the Past 87
Who I Am 97
White Christmas 107
Rebirth 109
Do Not Be Afraid 117
    The Root Goal 119
    The Sacral Goal 120
    The Solar Plexus Goal 120
    The Heart Goal 121
    The Throat Goal 121
    The Third Eye Goal 122
    The Crown Goal 122

And the Truth Shall Set You Free 123
Fast Forward 133

Author's Thoughts

What's your Fantasy?

When I first started writing, I was a bumbling mess. However, airing emotions with bad typing is not a bad thing. It's the first wave of releasing stories that are embedded inside of you. The more you write, the more comes out, and before I knew it, in less than a year, I penned the first drafts of what would be an autobiographical account of not only my past, present and future but what I was seeing for the country and her people at large.

I learned by trusting the process. I wrote what I was hearing, and I published it. Then I went out and actually lived it. Most people, when they think of a fantasy, almost immediately turn to sex, where a fantasy can be anything you dream of doing, but you're not really sure how you will obtain it. It's so out of the box that it's hard to imagine some things, but that is what I did. I took everything I've always fantasized about doing and wrote it all out inside of a story. Then, miraculously, they began to manifest. I met people who I had no idea existed. I got their names, their stories and their locations. All the while, I thought I was just making it all up.

When I first started all of this, I was coming out as a psychic medium. I was just beginning to finally understand who I am. All my life, I had been told that there was something wrong with me. I have been called "psycho," "crazy," "bipolar," and, one of my personal favorites, "a loose cannon" when, in reality, I was both gifted beyond what even I could comprehend and methodical with my plans.

Writing and publishing my books set everything in motion in my life. I talked about fantasies. Well, one of my biggest fantasies was to change our corrupt, inept and special interest-driven political system. I have for years, viewed it as a complete failure. The question began at home.

I had originally asked at the beginning of this book why my husband and I were so dysfunctional as a couple. For starters, my husband was a Democrat, and I was a Republican. We were brought up with two different styles of thinking embedded into our core beliefs. We are each born male or female -- not Democrat or Republican, yet we are told that we are either a Democrat or a Republican based on what our parents believe. We were raised with a false sense of what we actually are. We were indoctrinated, and it took us a long time to find out that we were a combination of both. Yet, the war between the two parties is only a war for our politicians' benefit. As long as WE, the People, are too busy fighting among ourselves while working and taking care of our families, it leaves little time to actually figure out what our elected "leaders" are up to.

Being a psychic medium while also being a massage therapist in Wilmington, Delaware (the corporate capital of America) often put me around the movers and shakers. I was known for being an intuitive massage therapist with a keen ability to go right to the spot of pain in the body and release it. What I didn't know I was doing for a very long time was that I was actually reading the issues/secrets that were, more often than not, the manifestation of what specific memory was really bothering them, and it was my job to release the pain that came with it. The truth is I did not need to massage to know any secret. More often than not, a handshake, a kiss on the cheek or a simple look into the eyes is usually enough for me to see. Once I started learning political secrets and having them confirmed, I took that as my sign to retire and move out of Delaware.

The war between the left and right only serves those in power. We are only viewed as the pawns in a game inside a deceptive machine called "government" that is fueled by the blood, sweat and tears of the people it was supposed to protect.

I see our outmoded "two-party" political system as bipolar and dysfunctional. We are caught inside of a protracted conflict that shifts every two years with each election cycle, keeping us in a constant state of turmoil. It is the system that is designed for constant agitation and stress to keep us down and prevent us from reaching our highest potential in an institutionalized hall of mirrors.

My second book was based on one question: "What would I do if I were President?" So, I wrote what I would do. Then, I sold my house and toured the country, selling my *Stimulus Package*. I was in Las Vegas in December of 2019 when I got sick. We packed up and headed back to Delaware. My granddaughter was born on Valentine's Day, and by March, we were being asked for two weeks to curb the pandemic. I knew then the reason why I had written my plan the way I did.

Kathy S. DeMatteis

By May, I had contacted the **Independent Party of Delaware** and spoke with Secretary-General Wolf von Baumgart. Shortly thereafter, I started my campaign for Governor of Delaware. It took seven weeks to open my campaign bank account. I received two donations when the bank suddenly and arbitrarily closed my account. So, I learned that the fastest way to end a campaign is to close its bank account. There is a state election law that requires every candidate committee to open a bank account. Had I won, the Delaware political establishment could have moved to nullify my election due to that one law apparently having been broken according to the setup. What I learned is that if the establishment doesn't want you in, they know who to call to get you out.

The only way around it is the write-in ballot, which must ultimately come from the People. According to our constitution, in order for a write-in candidate to take it away from a regular Democratic or Republican candidate, they must obtain fifty-two percent (52%) of the vote in order to do it. So, how can you get a fifty-two percent vote for a write-in candidate? Fear is what was used to get eighty-one percent of the population to take an unproved experimental vaccine. What is the opposite of fear? Love. How do you get a fifty-two percent majority to vote for Love instead of Fear? It is a basic process. Once you, as an individual, believe that you have been played and know you have been tricked, it becomes easy to make a fundamental political *paradigm shift*. I always love to quote Jeff Dunham's Peanut character: "Once you go purple, you never go back." As it turns out, independent / alternative awareness is growing by the day as the majority of the people struggle with high inflation, economic insecurity and a lower quality of life due to political corruption and government mismanagement. There has to be a better way, but we won't get it as long as the "donkey and elephant" political establishment remains in power, and the choice is ultimately up to you.

My other fantasy was to live in a place where love was the foundation. I wrote about a place called The Center of Love. It was an imagined place, and I wrote down everything that I was seeing in my mind. Six years later, most of what I wrote materialized; however, there are still some things that have yet to come to fruition. Names of characters in my books turned out to be the names of towns in Northern Maine that I found when I came to look at a property my son later bought to farm.

I got to live through the characters that I created, not really understanding that I was actually channeling and watching it all materialize. It has been the most amazing experience of my life.

When I published this book the first time, it led us to an opportunity to audition for a role in a movie being filmed in Las Vegas with Shonta Gibson (now deceased) and Eddie Bell based on their homeless experience. My character's name was Kat. That experience paved the way for me to write my second and third books.

It was my plan to solve not only the homeless problem but what I see as a flawed system. I have been extremely blessed to be a witness to the magic that we only ever really see inside of a Disney movie. That magic really does exist. There is an energy to it that is unlike anything else I have ever experienced. The other day, I was watching Frozen with my granddaughter, and as I sat there reading all the credits at the end, the very last thing I saw was video piracy. It clearly stated that stealing the movie affects the economy. The light bulb grew brighter that day. There is so much merchandising that comes from a movie. One only ever needs to visit Walt Disney World to know that.

I know the grip on this country, and I know many of the people who have tightened the noose around our necks. I've been at dinner parties where they joked about the shovel-ready jobs that were not so shovel-ready, and I was furious. This reminded me of the time when I was nineteen years old, taking care of my dying grandmother, when the agreement (made behind closed doors, sent our jobs out of the country. I looked at my grandfather and said, "Great, now I am going to have to fix this." I did not know it at the time, but that started my wheels in motion to begin learning. I dove into the alternative healing arts which -- let's be clear on this -- was the only health care system in our existence until major medical care and insurance was born a little over a hundred years ago. I set the intention to create all-inclusive healing centers.

So far, the farm has been established to provide farm-to-table all-organic, free-range meats and poultry, as well as providing the fats and goat's milk that is used inside of my soaps. I did not know how it was all going to happen. I just wrote what I was seeing in my head, playing out like a movie in my mind, and then, one day at a time, piece by piece, things began to fall into place. The real catch here is I did not do all of this for me to be a millionaire. That was not the point. The point was to affect billions of people and show them how to get out of a corporate mindset and take them to a higher way of thinking. I have found the best way to get someone to learn is through experience.

My books are completely merchandised, and it is my goal at the end of the day to secure a deal with Amazon that brings not only the distribution of my books to the world but also the products that I have been manufacturing in small batches inside my kitchens since 1997. It is my goal to obtain the lake property by the end of this year and to lay down the foundations for what will be the future of living. When you purchase this book, you help me secure the land.

You see, so far everything I have done, I have done it all based on faith, using my own money and donations from the community in which I live. I did not take one business loan. The definition of an entrepreneur is a crazy person who risks their own money for freedom instead of exchanging their freedom for money. I'll take the title of "crazy" and whatever else they want to call me, and I am good with it all. I did not do all this because I was upset over being called a name. I did all of this because I am a mother and, more importantly, a grandmother, and I have a whole bunch of babies who deserve to live a life in love.

This is why I did it and will continue to do it. I am an Independent, and we never give up; we just keep going until we get the job done. I never needed the title of President or Governor, and I just needed to do the job as if I were in order to benefit humanity.

Foreword

I had just entered a contest to win a B&B in Maine named the Center Lovell. It was my dream to have a B&B with a spa retreat, and this contest was my last-ditch effort.

When I was told to start writing this book, it came in a message from my Dad in heaven. I questioned him as to what I was writing about. He responded with, "How you won the Center, Lovell."

"Dad, I have not won the Center Lovell," I said. To which he responded, "Yes, I know. Start writing anyway." I wrote diligently all through that time as clue after clue of Maine appeared before our eyes.

When we did not win the inn, I was devastated and threw the printed manual and all my clues into my dresser drawer. Over time, my armpits were itching so badly, and I would walk around with a brush digging into my skin to relieve the itching that had manifested in me. The homemade deodorant I made had subsided the itching, and I thought I had solved my problem, but as time went on, the itching would happen again. I would wake up in the middle of the night scratching at my armpits until they were red.

One morning, I heard my dad reach out from Heaven again with a message. "Start writing again, Kathy," were the words he sent to me. I devoted all my time to it when I started writing this time. I was obsessed with writing. I wrote so much that it consumed my days and nights. I wrote in so many directions, from self-reflection to poetry to fantasy.

I loved writing and it seemed my whole life was changing. The more I wrote, the more my family wondered what happened to me. I was in love with writing and the writing bug caught me big time. As the winter months passed and my fingers flew across the keyboard I began to notice a lot of things change in me. The first and most noticeable was my armpits no longer itched. To this day, I have no more insatiable desire to claw myself raw under my arms. I truly believe the itch was my words itching to get out. The only way for it to happen was for my fingers, which are connected to my hands, which connect to my arms, which lead to my armpits, to start writing.

The more I typed, the more I released. Memories and clues to my past came out as my mind would remember parts of me buried underneath my skin. It took almost nine months of intense writing, with many emotional breaks. Sometimes, for weeks, I would look at the computer, unable to bring myself back to it. This time, it was not my dad that brought me back to finish this last part. In the end, I had to muster my willpower on my own.

The truth is that I was desperate for a new life. I could feel a part of me dying inside, and I was unable to figure out what part of me it was. At the same time, had I received what I was looking for, it would have been disastrous.

Had Conrad and I won the Center Lovell, our marriage would not have survived another year. I had all the skill set to run a place like that, but my marriage did not. I was so focused on my dream that I was failing to see what was right before my eyes. It took losing the contest to lead me on a journey to heal myself and, eventually, my marriage. I began to ask myself some big questions.

Why are we so dysfunctional as a couple?

When I asked myself that, I was asking my higher self to show me how to solve our marital issues. This turned out to be a question I would ask all throughout my relationship with my husband, or with anyone else for that matter.

Why are we so dysfunctional as people?

Many times, for the sake of my partner, I held back what I felt I should say or do to serve my partner's highest good. But when I held back my thoughts or my feelings on something, I was denying myself my true feelings. In many cases, I put myself in precarious situations and I grinned and bore it. I bit down and held my tongue, hoping to elude a bigger argument. I took the higher road in hopes of an offering of peace within the relationship when, in all reality, I was denying my true feelings.

My career as a massage therapist has always been to solve the core issue of how pain is manifesting in the body. This desire to rid the body of pain led me to a higher journey within my marriage to solve the issues we were having as a couple. As we journeyed together to find deeper understanding it led us on a course of deeper healing within each other.

We are a sensitive people. My relationship with my husband is the most complicated and glorious relationship I will ever have the pleasure to encounter. We are learning our way with each other. The blessing happened when I reached the moment when the light bulb went off, and I understood my partner. When I understood and respected his point of view, we then worked to find common ground…to meet somewhere in the middle.

This journey to this discovery did not happen overnight. Many modalities that were a part of my career I brought into my marriage, and we gave to each other in many ways. We started with massage and moved to body scrubs, body wraps, and facials. We began to notice how glued together as a couple we were. Even in our worst fights, when we both were ready to throw in the towel, there was something there that would not let us do it. I had to get to the truth of myself first and learn who I am. I had to learn how to shine with the gifts I came into this world with. I had to accept and embrace *myself*. I had to learn not to worry about what other people thought about me. I can't please the whole world and make everyone happy; it's impossible. I had to learn how to make myself happy—a very impossible task when you've spent your whole life pleasing other people. To try and break my mold of unhealthy patterns was something I had worked on for years with therapists and counselors.

It was not until I added Reiki healing into my practice that my life began to change. As a couple, we began to use Reiki on each other and noticed changes in how we would react in situations. I believe it was the culminating effects of everything we practiced as a couple that opened up the doors for deeper healing within ourselves.

Now, about this book. It is with great enthusiasm that I am sharing my mid-life crisis with you. I almost walked away from the love of my life in search of myself, while he almost left the planet to escape his pain. Together we began a journey of healing each other that has left our marriage in way better shape than when we first entered it.

I love to teach people. I've been teaching my whole life, but I just floated in where I was needed and then floated out. This time, I am growing my own roots. I am claiming my own stake as the teacher. This book is about who I am as a person on this planet, my life experiences, and how they shaped me into the person I am today. If I'm going to be a teacher to the world I have to share what I learned on my journey.

Spellbound

As my mind wanders, I find myself in a lake of wonder.

I feel your kiss upon my lips and a jolt of thunder.

My hands linger up your chest; my heart is so untwined.

I feel you heal me with your love, a fate that is so divine.

As my body crumbles into your mighty arms,

I know I've found my charming prince to be forever mine.

As we take our rightful spot into the end of time,

know no matter where you are, I am only steps behind.

I am wearing robes of gold with diamonds at my feet.

A crown of crystals perching and flowers I do greet.

Kathy S. DeMatteis

My strong, mighty King emerges from the ground

and into my waiting arms, my love can be found.

You are my eternity we shall rule all through the time.

Forever in each other's gaze is a mighty long time.

All my love, my darling man, forever through the sands of time,
your Queen until the end.

Your kiss has left me Spellbound.

Forever in my eyes, I peek all through the curtains to find a love
so profound.

I have placed a spell on you my words are laced with gold.

Promises of kisses and a love yet to be told.

I have a tale of Maine to tell, in time, many more.

Like when we hiked up to the mountain or slept upon your shore.

Of all my memories, none are so dear

than when you took my hand and brought me near.

A love so rare and pure, nothing could sustain

all the lashes that came our way, we conquered just the same.

Acknowledgments

I would like to thank my husband, Conrad; with him, there would be no Center of Love. Thank you for fixing each page setup, walking me through highlights, and giving me step-by-step instructions on how to fix any issue with the keyboard. Forever homage to you!

I would like to thank my children for allowing me the pleasure of being your mother. Each one of you has had a special way of teaching me about love, and it's from the bottom of my heart that I love each one of you.

Uncle Russell, without your help around the house, this would have taken my lifetime. Without your keen memories of Bear Pond and stories, I would not have had the excitement to continue the journey to Maine.

Jessie, it has been rough and amazing all at the same time. It's been an honor to call you my friend. I love you. So much of me would never have been realized had I not met you. Thank you for helping me finish this book and showing me the other side.

Ward Whipple, my editor and, most important, a true friend. You came in and saved me just when I needed saving. Thank you from the bottom of my heart.

LaSean Shelton, my publishing Coach. You pushed me to realize my dreams and believed in my book. You held my hand throughout this whole process, and I am forever grateful.

Trying to gather my thoughts in a cohesive manner to send my message to the world has been the hardest thing I have ever attempted to do in my life. When I set out to write this book, it was not because I had this driving force to do so. I was the kid who called out of school, avoiding book reports. What got me started was my dad, the same dad who made me sit at the table and do a book report on the state of Delaware when I was young. The same table now sits in my dining room, bellowing out to me to finish what I started.

If it were not for the angels reaching out to me from all corners I might have never finished this. My anxiety had reared its head again, and I found myself wanting to just drown. All my doubts about myself and who I am came crashing back. I found myself in a pit of despair. Every bad thing I have ever thought about myself came upon me, suffocating me at every turn until I had cornered myself into my home. Wanting desperately to escape but unable to find the strength. Afraid that the same forces would tunnel their way back into my head, defeating me at my next turn.

What is the message I want to send? What is it that I am trying to say to the world? Well, for starters, if I could don a superhero cape, I would come down and save everyone I could. That is my worst and best gift. I love to help people. I have learned so much from each experience, so I can't say it was bad. Everything works for good; it just sometimes takes a while to see the good when you are swirling in the bad. What I want to do is to show people that, first I am human.

This planet is made up of all kinds of different people with different ways of viewing the world in which we live. Some of us came here to be doctors, lawyers, and accountants. I came here to help people navigate the experiences of life. The only way to know the experiences is to live it.

This book is not for everyone, and I don't expect the whole world to fall to their knees at my feet, approving of what I wrote. This will find the people who need it. This book is about my experiences with life and how I learned how to navigate it. I am only telling you my story in the hope that something in my pages will speak to you. Maybe you will see yourself in the stories that follow and know that you are not alone. Maybe it will all sound like a load of crap, and you toss it aside.

Either way I have a dream, just like any one of you out there that has a dream. I almost gave up. I almost let the naysayers of the world push me back down. One thing I learned -

Your dream is your dream.

Can you imagine where we would be without people like Henry Ford or Thomas Edison? I would not even be on this computer without people like Bill Gates.

Never let anyone squash your dreams. You never know when it is going to happen. One thing is for sure: if you give up on yourself, expect to be disappointed.

About The Author

Kathy is a proven psychic medium who has spent her life trying to understand and embrace her psychic abilities. Having the ability to see the past, present and future, Kathy has used her unique gifts to bring peace to others while also learning how to improve her own life. She wrote this book in an attempt to help other people recognize their gifts and to help others embrace their natural intuition.

Foot Prints

Every Saturday, my grandparents would have a lunch of ham and cheese on rye bread for our whole family. I was about thirteen years old, and as I sat on the floor playing, I looked up at my Aunt Debbie and blurted out, "Yep, you're pregnant."

I was drawing circles in the air and gesturing to lord knows who when I looked at my Granny Sloan and confirmed in my mind she was expecting. I put my aunt on the hot seat. In front of the whole family, she had to confess that she was indeed pregnant. A massive argument exploded over my aunt not being married, and my whole family was screaming at each other.

Later that day my Granny asked me how I knew what I said.

"I just knew it," I told her.

She shared with me the story of when she had a visit from a young man who was recently deceased. She explained that I was special but that people would not understand me and I needed to learn to keep it to myself.

Kathy S. DeMatteis

I grew up in Old Mill Manor, in a brick ranch house that sat high up on a hill surrounded by brick walls. I lived with my mom, dad, and younger siblings, Jessica and Sherry. My mom, Joanne, worked part-time at a deli, and my dad, Bill, was a State Police Trooper. We knew we had an older sister, Renee, who had just started visiting us at our house. My bedroom was in the basement. The house was under construction and there were no formal steps to get to my room. There were only two ways to get there; one was an aluminum ladder to climb from my room to the kitchen. The second way was going through the door that led out to the garage.

In the wee hours of the morning one day, I woke to the sound of footsteps walking down steps that I knew were not there. I listened to the footsteps walk down the side of the basement next to my room. I heard it go through the wall, and then the footprints proceeded to walk right up to the foot of my bed. I knew it was my great-grandfather on my mother's side, known as Bumper. I was so scared that I wouldn't even reach over to my nightstand to get the phone to call someone for help. I stayed awake for hours until I dared to reach for my phone and call a friend of mine who talked to me until I heard my mom up in the kitchen. I climbed the ladder into the dining room that led to the kitchen where my mom was starting her day. I told her of my ghostly visitor, but my mom reassured me that it was not Bumper and that he would not try to scare me. But I can tell you that it *is* scary when you know someone has passed on, yet you see them at the foot of your bed.

What did he want? What was I supposed to do?

I remember feeling as if I was crazy or something was wrong with me when I told people what I saw. I really felt that I had no one I could talk to about what I was experiencing. I tried to tell others, but they just thought I was lying. Around this time, I decided to start lying to people about things that I was encountering. I remember the feeling of *wow, they bought that load of crap?* This happened for a while, but one day, I decided I just did not want to lie about things anymore, so I stopped.

I remember sitting in my science class at Christiana High School when I began to feel real panic. I had no idea how to handle what my body was feeling out of nowhere. As I breathed into the paper bag the teacher had given me, it felt like I was dying. An ambulance was called, and I was taken to the new hospital that had just opened, where I was diagnosed with Panic Disorder. I was given some Valium—which were little yellow pills with a "V" stamped on them—for me to take when I felt the panic start to come on.

Time passed. Our family was awaiting the arrival of my baby sister. On December 14, 1987, the newest addition to our family was born. My parents named her Amanda Rose. Within a day, the doctors were telling my parents that something was wrong. Amanda had something called Down Syndrome, an extra set of chromosomes that rendered her mentally challenged. My mom and dad explained to us girls as best they could that we would have challenges ahead, but we would see it through.

My dad was always tough on us girls. We were a cop's kids, expected to behave in certain ways. I told Dad the morning we went to bring Mom and Amanda home that she was special. That she was sent to save him and that he had to treat her differently than how he treated us girls. I told him he had to hug her and kiss her and make sure she knew she was loved. My dad was not a touchy-feely kind of dad. Sure, you always knew you were loved, but he didn't do it with his words or with a loving arm wrapped around you.

Kathy S. DeMatteis

Having Amanda was like having my own baby doll and the apple of my eye. I bought my very own car seat so I could take her with me to places in my car.

In June of 1988, I graduated from high school. I had been working for a home healthcare agency at the time. Still waiting to start my dreams of culinary school, I took a second job at Van Scoy Diamond Mine to save up. One day, I was selling a piece of jewelry to a woman who refused to put it on her fingers, and she asked me to try it on for her. It was a stunning blue sapphire in a marquise cut surrounded by 26 diamonds in a solid yellow gold band. As soon as I held my hand up, I knew I had to have it. That night I used my American Express card to put a $200 deposit down and ordered the ring. I had told myself I would make payments until it was paid off. In a week, the ring arrived, and I could not wait. I went to the bank, where I had a savings account with my dad as a guardian. I took the money out and paid my ring off in full. Excited about my purchase, I came home and showed my mom. The ring looked amazing on me. My father was furious with me that I would have spent money on something so frivolous. The money was for culinary school, but I justified my purchase by saying it was a graduation present for myself.

In November of 1988, I found a job that paid more money at a radiologist's office and I quit working at both my previous jobs. I was now commuting to North Wilmington, about 20 minutes from my parent's home.

My main supervisor was a tall woman with short gray hair. She took me to her office and told me I was not working out, but if I agreed to a date with her, things could be rearranged. I went to my immediate supervisor and explained the situation. I then came home and told my dad what happened. He reassured me that I must have misunderstood.

I went back to work the next morning. The tall lady wearing the gray suit took me back to her office. She put her hand on my knee and started to rub my leg. I immediately jumped up and ran out of her office, down the steps, passing the doctors in the hall. I grabbed my purse and out the door I went.

Eventually, I went home to tell my father I did not have a job. I had just bought a white Honda Civic, and my car payment was $219. I needed work, the loan was in my dad's name, and I could not screw him over.

That Saturday at lunch at my grandparents' house I explained to my uncle what happened. He offered me a job as a flagger for an electrical company that built power lines, and I accepted.

It was February, and the weather was very cold. I was driven out to the Delmarva Power utility yard and instructed to wait in the winch truck while it was being loaded with poles. I watched as the men walked around, securing the equipment. The truck would shift and bounce as it was lifting poles. It reminded me of amusement rides.

A man hoisted himself up into the driver's side. As soon as I laid eyes on him, I knew he would be the father of my children. I couldn't stop looking at his big, brown eyes. His name was Dennis. We drove to Centerville, where I was instructed to hold up a sign and tell cars to come or go. On our lunch breaks, we would sit in the truck and talk. He told me the story of when he was shocked with 7200 volts of electricity and felt himself walking down a tunnel. He told me he felt great peace and that he was content with following the energy in front of him. A woman walked up to him that he did not recognize and said, "It's not your turn. You need to go back."

I was fascinated by his near-death experience, and I wanted to know more about him. In the weeks ahead, the job was done, and we moved to the next site in Old New Castle. One day while we waited in the truck inside the parking lot of the church I attended as a child, the foreman gave the sign to leave for the day. As soon as we belted our seatbelts together, our eyes locked, and we kissed. I felt fireworks go off. He must have, too, because he backed the truck up into the pole behind us.

He picked me up that weekend and took me to his home in Laurel, where a dozen red roses were sitting on the kitchen table. I instantly felt like I was home. I married Dennis that October, and by July, after two weeks of being overdue, a C-section was scheduled, and we brought our baby home.

Over the course of the next year, I began to develop a close relationship with my husband's grandmother, Alberta. She lived in a little tin can trailer along the side of Route 24 in Laurel. A tiny woman with wide-rimmed glasses, it had been years since she had bathed or groomed, and you really could not get close to her—the smell was overwhelming.

One day, while driving home from the grocery store, I noticed her talking to the mailman outside in her driveway. Her robe had ripped to the point that her breasts were exposed. I just could not look past what I was seeing. Pulling into her driveway, I hollered, "Alberta, let's go to lunch!"

She was excited and got into my car. As I pulled out of the driveway I instead headed in the opposite direction of town and toward my home. I told her I could not take her into a restaurant looking how she did. I needed to get her cleaned up first. I helped her navigate the steps to our home and brought her to my bedroom, where a garden tub stood in the middle. As I began to take her clothes off, the stench was unbearable, and I vomited all over myself. I opened the windows and put the fans and air-conditioning on. I poured bottles of shampoo and perfumed soaps into the water, anything to mask the awful smell that had consumed my home. I had to cut her shoelaces off. Her toes were encrusted with years of dead skin, and her underwear was matted to her body as newspaper clung to her private parts. I helped her into the tub and tried my best to clean her up. I contacted her children and informed them where she was and that I would be keeping her until her home was cleaned and she had medical treatment.

Alberta stayed with us for a few months until her house was ready to go back in. During that time, she got established with a doctor's office, and it was set up to have home health aides go to her home.

Going Back Home

I was miserable living in Laurel. The only thing that I loved about it was picking strawberries in Sharptown, Maryland. Aside from that, I wanted to move back to Newark and be with my family again.

We started to talk about moving north to be closer to Dennis' work, and one day, while grocery shopping, I saw this beautiful green Victorian house for sale. I just loved it. I told Dennis that if he bought me that house, I would stay in Laurel. He told me he did not want a house with stairs and that he would not buy the house. I stood firm and said that I was not staying in Laurel without the house. I needed a new plan, which was beginning to take shape unbeknownst to me.

My Granny was from a small town called North Turner in Maine. She married my grandfather when he was discharged from the Navy. Eventually, they moved to Newark and bought a house in Meadowood, where they raised six children. In late 1969, my great-grandparents bought a camp on Bear Pond for the family to come and visit. The house was signed over to my grandparents in

1976 as an anniversary gift with the stipulation that it would be available to all family members.

Over the years, I spent every summer on Bear Pond. It was my favorite place to be. When it was time to will the property, my parents did not want the camp, and it was willed to my Aunt.

In the fall of 1991, I received a phone call that changed the course of my life. I was asked to take care of my grandparents Sloan back up in Newark. My granny was dying of emphysema. They would pay my living expenses if I cooked, cleaned, and took care of them.

With Dennis commuting two hours every day from Laurel to New Castle, we had been looking to come up north again. I grabbed at that chance to get back up to Newark. Overnight, I was packed, and I awaited her arrival by plane from Maine.

I was so gifted to have spent the last few months with my grandmother. Many nights, we would sit in her bed and talk about life. I learned how she liked her food prepared, and we had those deep moments. I washed her and got her dressed. I took care of her needs. I was paying her back for all the things she taught me. I had already learned how to decorate cakes from watching her as a child. She taught me how to sew clothes. She was a major role model for me and has always been a large part of who I am today.

By late January 1992, Granny's health was rapidly declining. Our room was next to hers, and I would listen to her pant for breath and cry out to God. I would lay there and cry and pray that her suffering would end. She struggled so much just to breathe. That night, I decided I hated cigarettes, and I swore I would never let my children smoke them.

Granny would start to see people that had passed walking around the house. One night, my sister Jessica walked into the room, and Granny said to her, "Aunt Pauline, I have not seen you in years."

I looked at Granny and said, "That is not Aunt Pauline; that is Jessica."

"You damn fool, I know Aunt Pauline when I see her," she said.

One morning in early February, she woke up feeling fantastic and walked down the steps by herself. She wanted to make her breakfast of soft-boiled eggs, and she did. She kept telling me how good she felt. It seemed like a miracle and that she was getting better. I went to Laurel that weekend to check on our trailer, which had yet to sell, and I received a phone call that Granny was not doing good and was put in the hospital. We immediately came back home, and I went in to visit her. It was February 9th, and as our family gathered in the room, I told her, "You're coming home tomorrow; you don't want a birthday party at the hospital, do you?"

Early the next morning, around 6 am, I received a phone call from the hospital asking us to get there right away. "I have my elderly grandfather and an infant at home. If my grandmother has already passed, please let me know," I told the nurse.

The nurse replied that she could not tell me that. I went upstairs to tell my grandfather that we must go to the hospital. I called my mom and told her to get over there. "It's a miracle; my mom is healed," she said.

"That's not what you are going to the hospital for; you have got to get it together," was my response.

I arrived and dropped my grandfather off at the door, where a man with a wheelchair picked him up. As I was walking down the hall, I heard the sobs of my mom and Aunt Debby. I walked into the hospital room, where I saw my grandmother's head tilted back with a tube down her throat. She had already gone to heaven.

Granny did go home on her birthday, February 10th, 1992. Her funeral was on the 13th. My sister Sherry's wedding was on the 14th, Valentine's Day. At the reception, it seemed, through my eyes, that Granny got to go out in style.

Sometime in March, I announced I was pregnant with my second child, and Dennis and I realized we would be needing our own home for our growing family. With my grandfather still needing care, my Uncle Russell agreed to move in with him as soon as we settled on a home. On October 22, I successfully labored and delivered my second baby boy into the world.

By January of 1993, we settled on a house in Brookhaven. It was centrally located, right in between my parents and grandparents Sloan's houses. That March, my husband was laid off, and within a few weeks, I found a job at Kmart. I began to sell jewelry again and had the best time on the microphone announcing the blue light specials. The stress of being laid off was taking its toll on Dennis, and he became extremely depressed. The stress of his depression was so heavy on my shoulders that I began to fall into depression as well.

One afternoon in late October, I saw a spirit out of the corner of my eye. I had seen these types of images two times earlier when I conceived my other children. I had already started contemplating divorcing my husband. I was miserable being married to him. When I saw this image, I thought perhaps this baby would save my marriage. I did not want to have a failed marriage; maybe number three would be the charm.

As time went on, our communication began to break down even more. I would come home from work after being on my feet all day to my two boys asleep on the floor. I would have to pick up my kids and put them in bed. I felt very unsupported in caring for my kids, and I did not understand why it was not a priority to have them in bed. I knew I would need a better-paying job than Kmart. I had no viable way of supporting my children on my salary, and I needed to come up with a plan. I began to think of different occupations that could pay my bills.

By December 1993, I was several months pregnant with my third child. One afternoon before Christmas, I was working at Kmart when it was announced a car was on fire in the parking lot. I ran outside, and to my horror, it was the car beside mine. I ran to my back locker, retrieved my car keys, and ran out to move my car. As my hands fumbled to get the keys in the ignition, I could feel a panic in me rise. I could smell the smoke, and it all flashed back to me.

The smoke is coming to take things away from me!

I finally managed to get the car started and moved it to another part of the parking lot. I was trying to get myself composed. I couldn't be crying at work.

As I was walking towards the entrance, a young man, tall with a full beard and blue eyes stopped me and asked me if I was okay. I just burst into tears, sobbing and hysterically crying. He wrapped his arms around me and hugged me. I just fell apart in his arms as all the memories of smoke and death poured out of me. I felt safe and secure, cradled in love, and I melted into his safety net.

Later that afternoon, we talked in the break room, and he introduced himself to me as Conrad DeMatteis. I thanked him for helping me and apologized for getting snot all over his smock. I felt so comfortable talking to him, and it felt like I knew him.

January arrived with tons of snow and bitterly cold temperatures as an ice storm blanketed the area. While I was at work I received a phone call from Dennis that I needed to come back home, as he got called in for storm duty.

"I just can't leave my job in the middle of a shift because you got called back to work," I said.

He informed me his job was more important than mine. I told my manager I had to leave work, and I came home.

As I turned out of the parking lot, a great madness came over me. I knew I would not be able to keep my job at Kmart and I resigned a few weeks later. On July 16, 1994, my daughter was born, and I scheduled a tubal ligation to be done the next day.

There were days when we seemed to be okay and days when I just could not bring myself to walk back through the door. A few months later, Dennis was laid off again and I went back to Kmart at nighttime and babysat the neighborhood children during the day. Within the next 18 months, my grandfather Sloan died, and our family dynamics took a dramatic shift. The Saturday lunch with our whole family was done.

Laying on of Hands

One night, at the jewelry counter, I experienced a blast from the past. Conrad DeMatteis walked in, clad in a pair of jeans and a blue button-down shirt. Seeing him filled me with excitement, leading to a long talk during which we caught up on each other's lives. He had gone to Del Tech to study auto mechanics and was acquainting himself with the nuances of fixing cars.

Our interaction soon grew frequent. Living only five minutes from his widowed mother, Conrad often dropped by Kmart to buy automobile accessories or birthday cards. Each time he came in, he made sure to stop by the counter for a chat.

One day, as a fellow associate and I arranged costume jewelry on the displays, I suddenly sensed Conrad's presence. On being asked how I knew, I replied that I could smell him. Within a minute, Conrad turned the corner, proving my hunch correct. Astonished, my colleague queried how I had known, to which I responded, "I don't know how I knew it; I just did."

By this time, Conrad's visits had become increasingly frequent, escalating to the point where he would join me in the lunchroom during my breaks. I found myself falling in love with him. I believed he was amazing, and if only the right girl had come along, she would have realized what a catch he was. With this in mind, I began introducing him to my friends, hoping for a spark.

Realizing that my survival and the care of my children hinged upon returning to school, I made plans. It was 1996, and my marriage was near its end, leaving me the sole caretaker for my three young children, aged two, four, and six. It was paramount for me to be there for them, necessitating a job with flexible hours.

I felt I would have more quality hours with my children to raise them if I chose the massage field over culinary, and that was the most important factor to me at this point in my life. My children are the loves of my life. I brought them into this world, and I felt I needed to nurture them. The demands of being a chef were high, and I felt massage was my best decision by leaps and bounds.

I have been massaging ever since I could move my fingers. I would massage my dad's ears and back for him when I was little. I would sit on my dad's back and rub this green witch hazel lotion on his back for hours. He had a little hand-held massager that plugged into the wall that I could slide my hands into. If we were driving in the car, I would sit behind him and massage his head and ears while he was driving.

When I worked at a home health care agency at the age of 16, I learned massage from a nurse named Elaine. When I asked her what that was, she gave me a description of what I would be doing. When she said naked people on a table, she lost me. I was done; in no way would I be rubbing naked people. It took about ten years for me to eat my words and change my mind.

I enrolled in Dawn School of Massage in Wilmington in the fall of 1996. My sister Jessica had enrolled in massage school as well; she went to school during the day, and I went at night. We each had two different sets of teachers and learned two different styles of massage. My class was a class of six, and one of my favorite partners to link up with was Craig. He gave the best massages, and on top of everything else, he was a drummer. The way he would body chop your body when he massaged was amazing. By this time, I knew Conrad played drums as well, and I would ponder the coincidences.

Two of my five teachers turned out to be major influences in how my career would turn out. Val and Robin were both friends from New York and had trained with a man named Patrick Collard. Both came from a more spiritual background, and it laid a foundation for me that, over the years, I have drawn from many times in my understanding of who I was. They talked to me about Shamans, Mystics, and looking for clues with body language.

Robin took our class to Delaware Park one day, where the lesson was to look at how people were walking and see if we could determine their occupation. Once we figured out why the body was behaving in a certain fashion, we then had to determine what therapy technique we needed to utilize to get the body to respond in the opposite direction and reverse it.

My takeaway lesson from that was to look in the opposite direction of what someone is saying or feeling, and in the opposite direction was the issue. I have used that technique for all my work throughout my career when dealing with pain in the body. Over the years, I began to put that same thinking into other situations and learned to solve problems sooner, or at least the ones I was willing to face.

As graduation approached, it was time to learn how to massage strangers. Val, our instructor, suggested we invite people in for free sessions. My first stop was at the Troop 6 State Police Station, where I brought in Dennis and also extended the invitation to Conrad. Dennis was the first to arrive. When I introduced him to Val, I said, "This is my husband." She questioned my statement, prompting a surprised response from me, "Yes, I'm certain he's my husband."

A few nights later, Conrad came in for his free massage. After meeting him, Val proclaimed, "Now that's your husband." Confused, I asked for an explanation; she mentioned my body language indicated as much. Conrad and I just looked at each other and laughed.

Once my maternal grandparents' estate was settled, my mother gifted each of us three daughters $1,000. I used my share to purchase an hourglass-shaped massage table with titanium legs manufactured by Oakworks. In less than a year, having finished school, I converted a room in my basement into a massage space, dubbing my practice "The Laying on of Hands."

The following year, Jessica and I opened a location on Kirkwood Highway in the Meadowood II Shopping Center. At the start of my career, I offered chair massages at banks and doctor's offices, gradually expanding to home visits. During this time, MBNA, the town's major bank, employed several of my clients. One executive, referred by Craig, proved particularly influential. Mr. and Mrs. Bee, in time, connected me with many of their friends.

Jessica was massaging part-time and working full-time at a bank. With her time restraints being what they were with a small child of her own, she discontinued massaging and left the practice.

By 1998, I had amassed so many outcalls and chair massage jobs that the need to rent space was not needed, and I closed the office when the lease ended.

With my massage license needing continuing education credits, I had signed up to take a Myofascial Release class at the Delaware School of Shiatsu. During this class, I had my first experience of someone trying to speak through me. I remember being at the table receiving when I heard my teacher, Ms. Jones, say, "We should come over to Kathy; she is getting ready to blossom." I wondered what that meant as she said it.

I was in a dream-like state. The first sensation I remember is a feeling of my lower abdomen being cut open, and I could feel the blood drip and the coolness of it against my skin. I knew right away I was back to July 7, 1990, and I was on the operating table having a C-Section to remove my son. I could feel the pressure in my lungs as they pulled him out of my birth canal. The next thing I remember is someone trying to speak through my own voice. I knew it was my great-grandmother Francina House. I became overwhelmed and hollered,

"I'm not ready for this!"

In a blink, it ended, and right away, I regretted that decision. I tried to make it come back to no avail. I booked a private session with Ms. Jones. She assured me that when I was ready, I would receive more information and that I could not rush this.

That summer, my neighbor Carla and I planned a day at the beach in Rehoboth with my three kids and her two. The currents were strong, and her kids got caught up in a riptide. She struggled to retrieve both of her children and once we were back on the beach, we all huddled together. We calmed down, but I noticed I could not find my daughter. I panicked and started screaming for her. I frantically ran up and down the beach, yelling, "The ocean took my baby!" Finally, a lifeguard brought her to me, and I swooped all three kids into my arms and marched off the beach.

During the following winter, I talked Dennis into letting me have a pool. I wanted an above ground so that I could feel safe. That April, the pool was delivered, and I was rooted to my backyard. I began to teach Massage back at Dawn School. I met one woman who was perfect for Conrad, and I set out to play Cupid. A few days later, I got a call from her, and she asked me, "Why are you not with Conrad?"

I said, "Because I am married to someone else."

Her reply was, "All you do is talk about how great he is, and all he did on the date is talk about how wonderful you are. When are you going to leave your husband and be with the man you love?"

I could not believe she said that to me. I was shocked, and I did not know what to say. Immediately, I called Conrad, and when he answered, I said, "Dude, how was your date?" He said, "It was an okay date, but the kiss felt like kissing my sister." I told him about the conversation I just had, and he asked me the same question…When was I going to leave him? I told him I was working on it.

Not What We've Been Told

March came in like a lion, and we received a phone call that Alberta, who had since been living in a nursing home, had passed away at the age of 91. Nothing could have ever prepared me for the next day's events.

On March 3, 1999, I was leaving a chiropractor's office in Hockessin when I looked up at the sky and knew something was different. When I pulled into the neighborhood, cars lined the street in front of my house. I thought nothing of this; my house always has cars because of the pool, and I just assumed a birthday party or something was happening. A few minutes later, I received a call from a neighbor across the street. She told me that the daughter of my neighbor two doors down had committed suicide by jumping off the Delaware Memorial Bridge. I remember falling knees-first onto the floor in disbelief.

Her five-year-old daughter had just left my house not even two hours previous. How could this be happening? I had just seen Amy a few days earlier as we waved to each other. We would take our kids out for ice cream and talk about life as we knew it. I knew she was stressed, but never did I think she would kill herself.

After what seemed like a million screams, I composed myself and looked to see what I could cook for the people who were gathering just two houses down. As I put a chicken in a pot of water, I heaved and sobbed. I chopped the onions and celery and put them in. As I chopped each ingredient and put it into the pot, I sobbed for her two daughters, her parents, and myself.

I placed some eggs, salt, and flour into a bowl and began to make noodles. I remember as I rolled the dough in between my hands how my tears fell into the batter. I don't believe I have ever cried so hard in my life. Her children were my kids' age; how could this have happened?

I pulled the boiled chicken out of the water, placed my noodles in the stock, and let them boil. I broke up the meat from the chicken and put it all back in the pot. I knew it was the worst pot of soup I had ever made in my life.

I took my attempt at comfort down two houses and knocked on the door. I just wanted to leave and run; I could not go in and feel all that pain. I could feel it so strongly from where I was at. I did not want any more.

A day later, her father called me and thanked me for the soup. He asked what I put in it and everyone raved it was the best soup they ever ate. I told him, "My tears."

Within a week, Amy's funeral happened, and I was in massive disbelief that she was dead. I could not believe it…nothing made sense to me. She did not feel gone. I could still feel her. I could see her smile. I could see her car drive past. I knew it was not right, what I was feeling deep inside. I knew that once I went to the church and saw her body, the proof would be there, and I could accept she was not there.

I walked into the church, and there was her closed casket with a spray of flowers over the top. I cringed, for I needed to know she was dead. I did not believe she was dead; I could still feel her; how could I feel her, yet she not be here? I had now been struggling with religion, for what I was being told at church did not seem to match what I was feeling inside of me.

One thing about a Baptist church that I love is the way they always end their service. At the end of Amy's funeral, the minister gave an open invitation to anyone who wanted to be saved. Just raise your hand, and they will pray for you. There was something about how heavy my heart was, and at that moment, my hand raised, and I was so grateful someone prayed for me.

A few weeks later, I had a dream.

I am walking back into the church for Amy's funeral. I walk right up to her casket. As I approach, the coffin opens, and Amy sits up and tells me, "Kathy, you need to investigate this; it's not what they have been telling us." I responded with, "What do you mean to investigate? What was I investigating?" With that, the dream ends.

In the beginning, I would go to the cemetery and just cry. I would ask The Universe what could have caused so much hurt that, in an instant, she would leave like that. I have always had questions that seemed to go unanswered, and this was the biggest. Why would a mother who adored her daughters leave them in such a way? The answer is easy and yet complicated: it was unbelievable pain.

Over the years, I have been witness to the dangerous effects that some prescription drugs have on our bodies. I have personal experiences that have changed my point of view on these things. Antibiotics have a horrible side effect on me, usually playing havoc on my system, so over time, I developed a fear of medicine. When I was young, I broke my leg, and I remember my mom trying to get me to take the medicine to help me with my pain. I completely understand her only goal was to help me with my pain, yet something inside me told me not to take that medicine.

In my early 20s, I began to develop chronic urinary tract infections. Knowing that the antibiotics would cause me more pain in the end, I was desperate for a different solution. I began to do more research and look for natural ways to clear up the UTI. I began drinking more water and drinking cranberry juice to keep my body better hydrated.

During this time of my life, I left my first husband, and over the year, I noticed a significant drop in infections, and overall, my body began to feel better. I had been learning about different ways to heal the body and had started to learn more about aromatherapy and its applications to the body. I began to pay more attention and started to ask the question why?

Why is the body behaving in this manner?

When I would massage someone I always had a knack for getting to the root of the issue with pain in the body. Now it was me who was experiencing issues, and I had to take that hard look to learn more about why my body was reacting in a certain way.

That summer I went on my first camping trip in the woods with my sisters and kids at Killen's Pond State Park in Felton. Every time I have camped there since, I have had experiences of a supernatural kind. On that night, I was asleep in my tent with my two youngest children. I woke up and realized I was hovering over my body. I could see my children and my body fast asleep. I quickly drifted above the tent, above the trees, and into the stars. The next thing I knew, I was in a room with my grandparents, Sloan, Alberta, and great-grandfather Bumper standing around a Cadillac convertible. Bumper began to walk towards me, and as I approached him, we embraced, and I said, "Oh, Bumper, I have not seen you in years," to which he replied, "I have not seen you in years either." I began to fade backward; I was back in the sky, back in the woods, and then back in my tent. It seemed like I was dreaming, but my memory of that night is as if it happened yesterday.

My career was heating up, and I was making connections with other business owners in my area. I started to meet other massage therapists and learn about other spa services that could complement my offerings, including body polishes and mud wraps. I started to work at Danne's Spa around this time. I have since learned lots of ways to give a body wrap, but my first time however left me wondering about my own sexuality when it was all done. If you have never been in a wet room before, picture a room about 12x12. The floors and walls are all tiled and sitting in the middle is a plastic table with a large plumbing system suspended down from the ceiling. Multitudes of showerheads seem to span off a central pipe, allowing water to flow out and through all the heads, hitting the body at various places. After one session and trying to completely cover up her body, I was left with soaking wet towels and sheets. I had to learn fast how to cover a body with as little as I could. It seemed that right away, I was breaching all the rules of proper draping procedures taught in massage school. Dead Sea mud is thick, and it does not come off with a simple spray of water. I had to use my hands to clear it. Her skin was so smooth, and as my hands glided over it felt amazing, and I was in love with it. When I noticed her nipples were fully erect and she was moaning, I realized I was way over my head. I did not know what to even think about myself.

I swore I would never work in that room again, for it seemed way too sensual. As luck would have it, I was scheduled to do a mud wrap on a man, and I wanted to die. I tried to beg the appointment off to someone else, but ultimately it was me. I was careful and super-cautious as not to touch him or not to even remotely enjoy what I was doing. In the end, he informed me that he was a State Trooper and was making sure no inappropriate activities were happening at this spa. I was grateful I passed the test, but that room was just too close for comfort for me.

There is something about how good the skin feels. I want to touch the skin, want to rub my hands over the silky smoothness and get lost in the sensations. I wanted the good feelings, but I needed to have a line drawn in the sand. I left that spa and began learning new ways to take products off. I began to teach massage and soon began teaching my students the things I did not have as part of my curriculum at the time. The school had a shower, and that, to me, was the safest way to take product off, not my hands feeling that soft amazing skin that wants to linger and explore the body. I was excited that I managed to find a loophole. I could give the clients what they wanted without feeling too much.

This Is the House That Love Built

I began dedicating as much time as I could to working. Not only did I cater to my private clients, but I also worked at the Hotel DuPont, a hair salon in Newark, and even taught at a school. In the year 2000, I negotiated a deal with a local nail school to develop a 100-hour massage program and teach two of the classes in exchange for Esthetician schooling. I built the program, which was subsequently approved, and by the summer of 2001, I had successfully taught the two classes and finished all my tests and exams. I was about to clock in my remaining hours when my teacher proposed a deal to help me finish up.

The deal involved writing an essay and constructing my future business plan. This essay birthed the early phases of a new dream on paper--a bed and breakfast integrated with a spa. This establishment was envisioned as a haven where love would be felt at the entrance, showcased by the fresh flowers on the table, picked as a daily gift to visitors. Guest beds adorned with a gift basket filled with sparkling wine, custom-painted flutes, body soaps, and chocolates would further enhance the welcoming ambiance. The love would also be tasted in the food, over which I prayed while preparing. Every detail was meticulously thought of, from the heart-shaped waffles served with maple syrup and homemade lobster ravioli in a pink champagne sauce to the freshly baked bread. What I penned down was a fantasy of a life with a new man in my most desired job and favorite place.

***

A two-story summer camp with over 6000 square feet and large floor-to-ceiling windows span the front of the house that overlooks the lake. A green roof made of steel, with cedar shake clapboards and a hand-carved sign over the front of the house. The living room is located on the main floor of the home. The fireplace sits in the middle, flanked with natural stone, and rises from the floor through the ceiling to the second floor. On either side of the fireplace sits an array of dining choices. On the side facing the kitchen is an old table and a set of wing-back chairs. On the other side sits a long dining table, and from this angle, you have a whole panoramic view of Bear Pond and Bear Mountain. The living room is dotted with winged back chairs and a card table where a game of chess has begun.

As you make your way closer to the lake, a series of Adirondack chairs encourage you to pull up a seat and take in the view. The back of the house, which runs along Route 219, has a small porch with the laundry, utilities, and a second powder room for the house. This wing has a bedroom for the caregiver of the property.

As you walk down the driveway you enter in through the main kitchen door. Along the right side of the living room is an L-shaped staircase leading to the second floor, one of the first-floor powder rooms hidden underneath her steps. The second-floor houses four bedrooms, along with innkeepers' quarters, each adorned with its own theme. A large porch spans the whole second floor, with sliders allowing each room to have its own private view of the lake, adorned with potted plants and small table and chair sets. A place to enjoy your morning coffee or take in a glass of wine and watch the sun set. Both suites – one named the Bottle Room and the other the Marble Room – are flanked on either side of the front of the camp overlooking views of Bear Pond and Bear Mountain. Both are L-shaped rooms with a master bath suite as well as a small private living room. The Junior Suites are along either side of the back end of the house. A spa with all the amenities is located along the side of the main building.

The Red Room is the heart of the home. The room has a round feeling to it, and in the middle sits a fireplace that opens, looking towards the lake. The bed is about five feet away from the fireplace, large and round and sitting low to the floor. Large pillows with elaborate prints of red, orange, and yellow adorn the landscape of the bed. The sheets are of red silk, the texture like cream to the skin. The floor-to-ceiling windows allow a massive view of the lake, heavy red tapestries on either side of the frame. It is the opinion of its creator to be a magical vortex of wonder that sees no boundaries. Each drape is hung, allowing you to stand and open the fabric with your arms spread wide, the sun setting in all its glory, showing beams of gold, orange, and fuchsia over the lake. The moon shines, bringing a brilliant cascade of lights as it plays off the glistening water.

***

This was the bedroom I built for Conrad and myself. This was to be the setting of my fantasies as I dreamt of a new chapter with the man I loved. I turned in my essay about my future business, procured my diploma, and submitted my application to the state to take my Esthetician Exam, which was set for September 24, 2001.

Kathy S. DeMatteis

Stirring events unfolded on September 11 as I sat in my living room, simultaneously watching the news and conversing with Conrad over the phone. He had joined the New Castle County police department. As we talked, I witnessed the second plane collide with the World Trade Center, and I found myself yelling, "We are under attack!"

My mind raced with fears for my children, who were not with me; my sons in Wilmington and my daughter in Newark were on opposite ends of the county, about 15 miles apart. Hysteria took over as I struggled to decide where to head first. I contacted my mother and attempted to impress upon her our imminent danger. She arrived shortly after, and we set off for the grocery store.

Throughout, I kept insisting, "We need to fetch the kids from school." Frustration gnawed at me for I couldn't fathom why she didn't understand the gravity of the situation, why we were shopping when people were perishing. As we headed home, the radio announced the attack on the Pentagon. My urgency intensified, and all I desired was to have my children with me.

Engulfed in panic about the undisclosed targets, I was near breaking point. Delaware sat right in between the attack sites, evoking a claustrophobic feeling of being increasingly boxed in. My anxiety peaked, echoing in a sharp pain that seized me as I stumbled over the impossible decision of where to go or what to do. The much-awaited early dismissal from schools finally yielded my children home within the next few hours.

From our house, the sound of planes from the New Castle County Airport, home to numerous military aircraft, was prominent. But in the shadow of these events, by noon, not a single plane split the sky. This bizarre quiet was immensely unsettling.

I put a chicken in the oven and invited my Aunt Debbie and her kids over for dinner. I just needed my family close by. We sat outside as the magnitude of what happened started to settle in. I had this sinking feeling: what if it were me that died today? My husband came home from work, and though I was happy that nothing had happened to him, he was not someone my heart wanted to comfort me.

The following weekend was Dover Downs race weekend, and I was getting ready to take my esthetician exam. Conrad had often helped me study for my tests. We sat as he read me question after question. With our shoulders touching, the desire to be closer was even stronger. I wanted to climb inside of his chest like that day in front of the Kmart. I just wanted to feel safe again. As we hugged and cried, we looked at each other; in an instant, Conrad uttered the words, "Screw it!" and with that, we started to kiss. I was back inside of his chest, back inside of where I wanted to be. This time, I did not let go.

I began to put my plan of escape together. I hired a lawyer and filed for divorce. I wrote down where I would live and how much money I needed to make. I went to Kmart and put on layaway all the things I would need.

In between all the planning, I melted down and placed myself in the Meadowood Hospital, where a doctor diagnosed me as bipolar. I was put on a medicine that seemed to put me in a fog. I was unable to comprehend how to do math, and trying to figure out how to bill for a large job where I needed to multiply figures seemed to elude me. I seemed to have an incredible amount of nervous energy, and my thoughts I could not focus. When I went back to the doctor and explained to him the symptoms I was having, he told me I was a "rapid cycler" and increased the dose I was on.

For weeks after that, my hands shook. I was unable to enjoy anything at all. If I was not depressed before the medicine, then by golly, they were making sure of it now. A few friends who knew me reached out to me, and I was referred to a psychiatrist in Pennsylvania who specialized in bipolar issues. After one visit with her, she explained to me that I was living with someone who was bipolar and that I was developing coping skills. She wrote me a prescription with the intention to wean myself off the medication.

In April 2002, I took Conrad to a B&B in Maryland called Elk Forge for his birthday. We discussed the idea of running a place like that together. We both applied to work there to see if we could handle working at an inn and spa. I worked in the spa while Conrad did light housekeeping inside the main house. We used this time to talk with the owners and determine if this was something we wanted to pursue.

I signed a contract for a two-bedroom apartment and moved in with my kids. It was located right across the street from my sister Sherry's house. In July 2002, my divorce was finalized, and I felt free. Conrad moved into an apartment building about a mile away from me, and we officially started dating in the eyes of our family and friends. There were many things we needed to learn, and one of the key points was being on the same page. We both understood the importance of being a united team.

In Delaware, one of the requirements for getting a divorce is taking a parenting class. We used the material from that class to establish a strong foundation between Conrad and me, ensuring that we would always be on the same page in our household. I had prior experience with parenting conflict between separated parents, so I knew it was crucial to get this right. Conrad and I made a commitment to work together as a team, with my children placed under our care. Initially, my kids were upset, feeling like I had put Conrad above them. It took some time to resolve this power struggle and establish a harmonious dynamic. Our goal was to always consult each other before making any major decisions, and we strived to honor that agreement.

We agreed to marry and set a date for ourselves. Christmas approached, and we agreed to spend our first Christmas with our prospective families and not be together. As our day lingered on, we regretted that decision. Later that night, when we got together, we talked and agreed that we would never spend Christmas apart again.

A few days before New Year's, I spent the night with Conrad while my kids were with their father. He woke up in the night with a terrible bug, and I went to the grocery store to get some pills to help stop his symptoms. He looked like death warmed over, and I took care of him.

The next day was New Year's Eve, and we were invited to a formal party at a client's house. I wanted to go to this party, as it was a good group of people to try and make some business contacts. We were thrilled about our first "coming out to the world" party as a couple, and to be able to do it in such a fashion was exciting. It felt like we were in high school going to the prom. I wore a gold dress that seemed to speak volumes for me. I felt beautiful, and I felt like I fit in with this crowd. We mingled and had a fantastic night. As the party went on, that flu reared its head, and I had to leave before the new year was rung in. We said goodnight to our wonderful hosts and exited through the main doors as the dance floor was being laid out. Conrad handed the keys to the valet driver, and I began throwing up in the front yard. I was so mortified I just wanted to die, and the way my body was feeling, at that moment, it was possible. Conrad took me to his home and cared for me the way I had cared for him a few days previous. He stayed with me and called his mother to inform her he would not be there for her New Year's Day party.

We began planning our wedding. Conrad's sister had just gotten engaged over the holidays, and he informed me the date we picked was right around hers. We had not told his family of our plans, and Conrad asked me to change our date, to which I agreed. We had started looking at places that we could rent, and with our leases ending both on May 31, we decided to make our wedding date June 1, 2003. My sister Shery and her husband had just decided to sell their home at Red Mill Farms and we agreed to purchase it. We settled in April of 2003 and decided it would be best for us as a family if we moved in all together at the same time.

We planned an outdoor wedding along the grounds of Brandywine Creek State Park. We married under a trellis filled with white lights and strands of wisteria. The birds were our choir, and the trees were our steeple. The day was miserably cold, with a light, annoying rain. They say if it rains on your wedding day, it is a sign of good luck. We were going to need it.

We honeymooned in the Dominican Republic on a topless beach. I loved it! For the first time in my life, I could walk down a beach half-naked. I sat next to a woman who, in contrast, was a much bigger woman than I. We talked about how amazing it felt to not have to cover up our breasts. I had a new sense of freedom, and I loved how it felt. We came home to start our new life together as man and wife.

One of the foundations we had instilled was learning to be in service to each other. We started off with simple things like washing each other in the tub or shower. Conrad loved to be massaged and often would ask me to massage him. Over the course of our marriage, I would massage him, but when it came time for me to get a massage, he would beg it off. He would tell me that he could not compare to a professional and wanted me to go see a friend for my massage. I kept trying to tell him that what I wanted was him and not a professional massage. I wanted his attention. I wanted from him what I was giving to him. I wanted to feel that love and have it mutual. My pleas for his touch were ignored, and I stopped massaging him. One day, he came to me and asked me why I did not massage him anymore. I looked into his eyes and asked him this one question: "Why do you think?"

He looked at me and said, "Because I don't massage you?"

It took Conrad a couple of days to process, and then he came to me and said, "Teach me to massage you." This embarked us on a mission that has spanned our whole marriage. This is what has saved us on every perilous road. It began with just once a month, then it turned into a couple of weeks, and then it was weekly. What we made a choice to do is to be in service to each other.

In February of 2004, Dennis's mental health deteriorated, and it was decided to sell the house in Brookhaven. Conrad and I had just received our tax refund and we used that money to fix the house up to sell. One day, while we were in the backyard looking at the pool, he asked me if I wanted to just sell the Red Mill house. We listed the house in Red Mill Farms and sold it a few months later with a nice profit.

Over the next few years, Dennis' mental health was plagued with the hospital after hospital and suicide attempts, and it seemed every week I had to travel up and down the state to help him get settled. The years rolled by, and dealing with three teenagers, managing a house and husband, and working my life seemed to just pile up. I worked mostly doing out calls and at a few spas where I worked part-time. My desire to have a B&B was getting stronger.

My kids were all getting older and learning how to drive. It seemed I was in the throes of parenthood and all the issues that went with it. Time was flying by, and it would appear I was on autopilot, pumping out massages, facials, and waxing, working as much as I could to support my family.

Superman

In December 2011, Conrad and I went away for Christmas in Rehoboth Beach and began discussing the possibility of finding our own inn. To keep his job secure, we needed a location close enough for him to commute. Within hours, Conrad found a former B&B in Dover that had been foreclosed and was in need of work.

Over the next three years, we looked at countless houses in search of our dream location. One property, which I called the "Port Penn" house, was as perfect as we could find. It had almost everything on our list and used to be a group home for handicapped individuals. The large six-bedroom wing built on the back would have been ideal for a spa. However, the house needed over $100,000 in restorations, and the trailer in the backyard made financing impossible. Fortunately, that home was bought, and now, it houses homeless veterans.

Conrad and I discussed all the problems we would inherit when trying to sell such a unique property. I remember telling him that we should just give it to someone like me—someone who had the dream but lacked the funds to make it happen. I must have driven my poor real estate agents insane.

The biggest challenge, which took me three years to overcome, was to not be emotionally attached to my current house. There were things I needed to let go of, including my pool. One day in April 2012, while we were coming home from Bermuda, my eldest went to mow the yard. The mower hit a buried kickstand, tearing a hole right through the frame and liner. Conrad suggested we take the pool down, but I refused. I loved to swim and be outside.

Over the next two seasons, every imaginable obstacle arose, pushing me to take the pool down—from green water and pinholes in the liner to the hoses falling off and emptying it out. After another challenging summer, I covered the pool, settling into the wait for spring to reopen it.

My dad had been diagnosed with prostate cancer years earlier and had undergone a procedure that left him in severe pain and dysfunction. He traveled to Florida to see a specialist who would "milk his prostate" to release the pus that had accumulated. He once asked if I knew how to milk a prostate and if I would do it for him.

All my life, I never said no to my dad. As a child, I made his eggs and tea, rubbed his back, and massaged his ears. When I realized what milking the prostate entailed, it was more than I could process, and I said no. I still cry to this day because my own fears of being labeled got in the way of me doing something I was medically qualified to do. My training as a massage therapist and all the rules regarding professionalism made me fear that this was something sexual or inappropriate.

The inability to function sexually as a normal couple put a lot of strain on my parents' relationship. I remembered that my grandfather had a botched procedure that rendered him unable to be intimate with my grandmother.

Conrad and I began experiencing similar problems. Aware of the strain it could put on our relationship, we set out to find solutions. We experimented with a testosterone gel, read about its negative side effects, and concluded it wasn't worth the risk. We explored other techniques to improve his function, from books on Kundalini energy to natural remedies. Eventually, we settled on using Cialis for planned romantic evenings.

Conrad had been seeing a heart doctor for some time. His father had died in 1974 of a massive heart attack, and the fear of history repeating itself was always in the back of our minds. In May 2013, my father had his first heart operation to repair a leaking valve. Initially, it seemed successful, but within a few months, it became clear it had failed, leading to a second surgery scheduled for December 12. Though the operation was successful, my father experienced seizures shortly afterward, and doctors struggled to understand the cause. Eventually, medication controlled the seizures, and he was sent home to recuperate.

The holidays came and went, and it became apparent that my dad was not improving. One morning, my mom and Sherry asked me to watch him while they went grocery shopping. I lived less than a mile away and found him on the floor, confused and trying to dress. I helped him into the recliner, massaged his feet, and we talked.

He told me he thought he was dying. I assured him it wasn't that day but admitted that it felt like it was soon. I asked if he had seen any figures around him, and he said he had seen images on the computer screen, but when he turned, they were gone.

Mom and Sherry returned, and I told them what had happened. Later, I met Conrad for lunch and received a call from Mom to come back. We returned to find the visiting nurse checking on Dad. I shared what had happened, and the nurse suggested he go to the hospital. In the kitchen, I asked Mom, "Don't you think it's time we call hospice?" She insisted on trying anything that could save Dad. Sherry and I took him to the hospital, where he was admitted. Though still able to talk a little, his condition deteriorated rapidly, and he began having seizures.

One afternoon, Dad pointed to the sky and said, "I see God," before having a terrible seizure. My sister Jessica, who worked at the hospital, called for comfort measures only. It was decided to move Dad to hospice, and I don't believe he spoke any more words afterward. He would moan or holler, but that was the extent of his earthly communication. Mom signed the papers, and we requested he be transferred home by ambulance. That was January 18.

That night, he was moved to the hospice wing, where Sherry, Jessica, my older sister Renee, and niece Pam stayed with him. My daughter and I stayed with Mom. The following morning, we relieved my sisters and niece.

I knew my communication with Dad was now happening in my head, subtly, like a knowing. I asked the nurse when the ambulance was expected, and she discovered none had been ordered. I insisted on correcting the error so Dad could go home as planned.

The summer before Dad's death, he had built a brick pathway leading to the backyard and the handicapped ramp he and my son had constructed. On January 19, around 4 p.m., the ambulance brought my unresponsive Dad home one last time. I talked to him, saying, "Dad, you're home, wake up," hoping his eyes would open.

Around 8 p.m., Jessica asked us to say our goodbyes and leave, believing Dad would make it through the night. I was relieved, not wanting to watch him die. I went home to relax in a bath, but received a call from Jessica to come back alone. Wearing my nightgown, I drove back. One by one, my sisters rejoined us, and we put on Dad's favorite Russian movie, "Life Is Beautiful," waiting for the night to progress.

I sat at his feet when I heard Dad say, "Kathy Sue, do you want to feel this?" I said yes and felt a sensation of compression in my body. It was a whirlwind of sensations and the presence of many people who had passed, including relatives from both sides of the family.

I fell into a trance, speaking an unfamiliar language and drawing symbols. Jessica helped calm me outside, asking me to send it away. Back inside, I lay next to Dad, holding his hand, waiting for death. A sensation, like a volt of electricity, passed into my hands, and my Superman was gone.

Dad's funeral and wake were held on January 24, 2014. Many spoke about his influence on their lives, but no one could follow my baby sister Amanda. When she said, "I love you from the bottom of my heart," there wasn't a dry eye in the room.

The wake was at my parents' house, perfect for large gatherings. We gathered in the living room, where the TV played SoundScapes. Between my mom and Conrad's mom, I glanced at the television. The artist was William Close, the song was

"Moving Between Worlds," and the album was Behind the Veil, 2013. I couldn't believe it—my dad had sent his first message from the other side. Elated, I quickly had Conrad take a picture.

My New Reality

In the weeks following my father's death, the events of that night replayed incessantly in my mind. For years, I had been trying to tell my family that something was different about me. Nothing made it clearer than when I began speaking in an odd language and drawing in the air while my father was dying. My family had no idea what had happened to me. It must have looked like I was losing it due to the grief of losing my dad. I was breaking apart, but not in a bad way—I was breaking open. I was trying to wrap my head around what was happening to me and the strange phenomena that now seemed pervasive: the smell of Old Spice cologne, sudden cravings for chili dogs, and chills that left me with a feeling of not being alone. I began reading up on ghostly visits and taking online tests to see if I could determine my level of psychic ability. Years ago, we visited a local medium. She threw her hands in the air and said, "You're already doing this!"

I simply stammered, "I know!" I just wasn't ready to deal with it.

In early February 2014, I had chosen to have an ablation and was heading to Christiana Hospital for the procedure. During the drive, I kept singing an old jingle from WSTW radio: "I'm a lucky girl, hoorah oh boy, look at my diamond, it came from Van Scoy. My boyfriend bought it and saved lots of money, too. Van Scoy, the diamond king, yes, he's the man for you." I remember waiting for the procedure to start; the jingle stuck in my head.

Lying down on the operating table as the doctors prepped me, I said, "Make sure I come back; I'm not done here." The last thing I saw was the large white lights above me, and then I was out. The next thing I remember was waking up.

By April 2014, I was seeking local mediums to explain what was happening to me. During my first meditation over the phone with a medium I was considering for training, two spirits entered my session: Tommy Van Scoy, the Diamond King of Delaware, and my ex-brother-in-law. I had met Mr. Van Scoy once during the Van Scoy Diamond Mine annual sale when I worked there years earlier. He wore a full-length coat and a gold crown with diamonds pinned to the breast. After the meditation, I took a walk. I spoke to Tommy in my head, promising to deliver his message if he showed me the crown. I didn't care how—a Budweiser beer commercial or the King of England—I just needed to see the crown.

A few days later, I had several appointments. One client was Tommy Van Scoy's son. Another client, the first on my schedule, was a young lady for a waxing. When I walked into the room and removed the towel from her midsection, there it was: a tattoo of a crown on her left thigh. I couldn't believe it. I started jumping up and down, begged her to let me take a picture, and explained that I was coming out as a medium.

Within a day, Tommy's son was in front of me. Nervously, I said, "I have a message from your dad for you," and explained everything, showing him the picture of the crown. He was initially shocked and unsure of what to think or say. Weeks later, at a wedding, he thanked me for the message.

The second spirit in the meditation was my ex-husband Dennis's brother. For weeks, I had been waking up to the smell of smoke. I would check outside, but there was no fire. Then, I got a call from a bank, insisting I was the contact for my ex-brother-in-law's mortgage. They had my home number and correctly spelled my name. I contacted my daughter for her aunt's phone number to relay that her late husband was trying to send her a message. When my ex-sister-in-law called the bank, the receptionist had to interrupt her due to fire alarms going off, confirming her late husband's presence. I was thrilled to realize I was accurately receiving messages from the spirit world, starting to have deceased individuals ask me to relay messages.

With a vacation to South Myrtle Beach approaching, I decided to start training with a group in North Wilmington, scheduling my first session for the first week of June. On the fourth night of our vacation, I was exhausted and went to bed early. Around 11 p.m., I jolted awake to see a tall figure in a black cloak, resembling the grim reaper from the Bible tracts my dad had when I was a kid. I knew it was death.

Almost hysterical, I tried to explain to Conrad what I had seen. It was not just the vision; it was the heavy, sinking feeling. Unable to sleep, I paced the hotel room and went downstairs to the pool to collect myself.

I eventually saw a woman in pain and offered to massage her in the pool, which she accepted. As we talked, the desire to go home gnawed at me, and I asked Conrad if we could leave. My friend Carla saw my Facebook post about heading home and invited us to a baseball game the next night. At the game, I saw Carrie, a friend of my friends, and immediately knew she was the center of my dream. I knew her husband Frank had heart issues and asked how he was doing, wondering why I had that dream. It felt like sitting on a nuclear warhead with no destination.

The game was great, and the fireworks were spectacular. I took several pictures and mingled, which helped distract me from the grim reaper dream.

A few days later, Carla called frantically, begging me to pray for Carrie's nephew, who was in the hospital. I instantly knew this was what the dream was about. Looking at the firework pictures, I saw three sets of bundled orbs, confirming my intuition. Carrie's twin brother acknowledged that their nephew was with their mother and not coming back as they gathered around the hospital bed.

In a few days, I would attend my first class to get some help. I didn't know why I was getting these dreams of death or what to do with the information. It seemed reckless to tell someone a random prophetic message without the full picture.

My life was changing, and I was conflicted about this newfound "gift" and the implications of being the bearer of bad news. I felt like an outcast, and now more so with this revelation. I couldn't wait to start training and learn to manage my new abilities. These waves of feelings came and went—sometimes, I felt like a computer receiving massive data downloads, which left me exhausted.

Managing this gift was challenging. It's not like learning you have cancer or diabetes; it's uncovering a buried truth about yourself and facing its ramifications. To reveal such a deeply hidden truth is difficult; it's self-judgment rather than the judgment of others. For years, I didn't believe in myself, making it easy for others to dismiss me. Coming out as a medium felt like coming out as gay—it was a monumental revelation.

Telling my story felt like trying to lessen the burden. I never fit in with my husband's family; I was the square peg trying to fit into the round hole. When my husband's deceased father woke me up one night, I knew the challenge of delivering the message would be excruciating due to the fallout.

My second significant experience happened on May 31, when Conrad's father brought his nephew Eddie to me in spirit around midnight. I woke up and asked Conrad, "Who is Eddie, who died in a car accident due to alcohol?" He informed me Eddie was Aunt Anne's son.

That Monday was my first development circle. I brought the dream to class, and the response was, "Deliver the message." On my way home, I stopped at Aunt Anne's house but found her grandson, who told me she was at a funeral. I called her later, and when she answered, I asked, "Did you try to get tickets to see Teresa Caputo in Wilmington?" She confirmed, shocked that I knew. I told her to sit down as I had something important to tell her.

When I revealed I was a medium, she started screaming. Summoning my courage, I said, "Your brother Conrad brought your son Eddie to me last night, and I have a message for you. Do you want it?"

She said, "Yes, how soon can you get here?"

It was a bit after 5 p.m. on a Monday. I navigated through the traffic near Christiana Hospital and the Bank of America Complex. Miraculously, I encountered no cars and made it to Aunt Anne's house in less than ten minutes.

We went to the kitchen, and Eddie delivered the message through me. Afterward, I asked her grandson for the package I had seen on the steps. Inside was a pair of shoe inserts. I said, "Aunt Anne, these are footprints." She excitedly showed me a large framed poster of "Footprints in the Sand," her favorite saying. I turned to her and said, "There is your validation. This was a divine message."

I had enough evidence that things were going to change. I decided to write a letter to my mom to give her a window into what was happening to me. This is the letter I wrote to her on June 3, 2014:

***

Dear Mom,

I'm telling you something that I felt I should share in this manner. From the time I was born, my father played a pivotal role in shaping who I am as a person. My first memory was, "Kathy Sue, do you want to learn how to make your daddy a cup of tea?" From there, it progressed to, "Kathy Sue, do you want to learn how to make eggs for your daddy?" It eventually became, "Kathy Sue, do you want to learn how to massage your daddy's back?" I did these things with great excitement; I remember that vividly. I know they were building blocks.

Over the years, I learned many more things from him. The night my dad died, he gave me the last lesson he could have given me on earth: to see, hear, smell, feel, and interpret the other side. None of these experiences would have been possible had you not chosen him. You picked the best man you possibly could to mold me into who I am supposed to be. Each breath on earth is poignant and meaningful. You've given me my purpose here on earth. Thank you.

Your loving daughter,

Kathy Sue

My mother's response:

How beautifully said. Maybe your gift is in writing. I always thought Dad was my soulmate, and I still feel that way. Otherwise, how else would I have gotten such wonderful children, each with their own special gifts? Life is a circle, Kathy, in more ways than one. Thank you for such a wonderful gift.

As always, your loving mother

***

About one week later, I awoke from a nightmare that felt eerily real, much like the one before. This time, it involved my son. Frantic and scared, I called his phone until he answered. He assured me he was alive, still at work, and that I shouldn't worry. The next day was my development circle, and when I asked my mentor, she said it was not my son but one of his friends. I felt relieved that it wasn't my son, but knowing most of my son's friends, the thought of not knowing who, what, where, when, and how was frightening. My mentor advised me to let it go, so I put it out of my mind and went about my life.

A few weeks later, I was washing some picture frames and fixated on Corey in one photo. It was our trip to Florida back in 2007, and we had allowed our kids to each bring a friend. I remember using my fingers to draw a circle around Corey's head as I asked him, "What are you doing? How is your life?"

I'm not sure how many days passed, or even if it was hours, but I do remember it was Sunday, June 22. I was in the kitchen cooking dinner when I suddenly shut off the burners and walked out my front door. There was Corey standing in my driveway talking to Conrad. I hadn't seen him in a while. He looked as handsome as ever, with his amazing hair and long eyelashes that enhanced his dreamy milk chocolate eyes. I asked him what he was doing, and he said he was down at the trestle; some kids were giving him a hard time, and he felt safer walking home this way. I offered him a ride home, which he declined. I persisted, and on the third time, he accepted. As we got into the car, I asked him to pull up his sleeves and show me his arms. He did, and when I saw one mark, he promised me it was old and that he didn't do that anymore, pleading with me not to tell his mom.

Corey then shared with me that he was having dreams that were coming true and how scared he was. I told him I understood what was happening and knew a therapist who could help him. I gave him a meditation to listen to and asked for his insurance information to arrange a session. As we arrived at his house, I told him I was a medium and could help him. His grandfather and uncle came down from the spirit realm, insisting he shouldn't make the same mistakes they had. I asked Corey if I could pray for him, and he said he would like that. We prayed together, hugged, and I kissed him on his cheek goodbye.

That was the last time I ever saw Corey walking and talking. He accidentally overdosed on heroin the next day.

The hardest thing I ever had to endure was seeing the heartache on my children's faces. I knew Corey was not coming home. I didn't think the Universe was making all the decisions and that he could change it, but I knew inside the wheels were already in motion. I went to the hospital with my kids to visit him. As we walked out, one light was dimming up and down. It felt like something was trying to get my attention. I looked at the light and acknowledged it in my mind, and with that, the light went back up bright. Corey was declared brain-dead on June 26, just a few days short of his birthday.

The fact that this young, amazing man is dead due to heroin just blows my mind. We have a major problem in this country with not recognizing what is and what is not a dangerous drug. At the time of his death, as a mom, I was super-concerned over my kids smoking pot. Knowing what I know now, marijuana was the least of my worries. In fact, marijuana is being proven to help people recover from their addictions, to treat PTSD, and to help heal people who suffer from cancer. In my mind, I started to question: why is this plant illegal?

Corey's funeral was beyond sad. No parent should ever have to bury a son. His family keeps Corey's spirit alive and flowing with a bike run that raises money to fight addiction. My private practice of massage and skin care was slowly beginning to turn into spirit messages, and Corey proved, over time, to be involved in many of them.

Transitions

I began to know Jaycee before I even saw her being born. One morning, I dreamt I was walking in a field that resembled the park where Conrad and I had gotten married. I was conversing with a child who appeared to be about seven years old. She is the granddaughter of my deceased Aunt Debby. Throughout most of her life, I have played the role of her grandmother, even though she is actually my second cousin. By the time Jaycee turned five, I was convinced that the child I had walked with in the field that day was indeed her. I remember her giggling in the back seat of my car as she talked to her brother Robert, who had passed away in utero—a baby brother she never knew existed.

As my life developed in the role of a medium, I felt a strong need to not only train with an experienced medium but also to start attending a prophetic church. This urge felt like it was led by my father. I shared my experiences and the messages I was receiving with the pastor. We discussed why I had been shown these images and what their purpose was. I struggled to understand why I had been shown something I couldn't prevent. The grief over not being able to stop Corey's death weighed heavily on my heart, and I sought refuge in the church to help me cope with my emotions.

In July, the church hosted an evening Bible School class that we thought would be beneficial for Jaycee, so we took her there for the week. On the second night, while in the sanctuary, I felt an urge to go out and rest in the truck. I lay down for what seemed like just a few minutes. When I awoke, I saw a figure that appeared to be Moses, dressed in a brown raggedy outfit with a long, crooked stick in his hand, standing right under a tree. I did a double-take and watched as the image disappeared right in front of me. I ran back into the church, searching for Conrad, and told him what I had just seen. Then, I sought out the pastor to see if he could explain what had just happened in the parking lot.

During this journey, I felt conflicted between what I was experiencing and what I was being told in the church. One morning, I received a text message from the pastor urging me to attend church the next day because a video message would be shown while he was on vacation. I replied that I would be there and added a message: "Is it not interesting that our bones are made up of some of the same materials found in the stars? I wonder why God did that—was it to help us navigate through the woods?"

That morning, I chose a different spot in the church. I started a conversation with a woman who showed me a bracelet made of gemstones. I complimented her on how beautiful it was and mentioned that I was planning to purchase some stones for my office. She asked about my occupation, and I told her I was just coming out as a medium. She seemed excited but warned me about crystals. Puzzled, I asked her what the difference was between her gemstones and crystals. She said they were the work of the devil. I stared blankly at her, nodding like a bobblehead doll, trying to process that information. I thanked her and turned away, thinking, "Wow, do people actually believe that?"

The program began to play on the screen, and as the pastor spoke, he talked about not looking to the stars for God. I thought to myself, "Did the wise men not follow a star?" I left the church knowing I did not need to return. I sent the minister a message, thanking him for helping me on my journey, and went on my way.

I started searching for a new church, looking for one with a more spiritual nature. As summer passed, I began working with a therapist to help me manage my emotions. I started to question whether the group I had joined was the best fit for me.

The 495 bridge was the fastest route to my development classes, but a construction company had dumped some dirt into the water, cracking the bridge and shutting down the route for months. Each week, I struggled to find a way to class without needing to prepare hours in advance. I hadn't formed any connections with the women in this group, and I felt like an outsider trying to peer in. I started attending séances and meditations, meeting a lot of people. I quickly learned that Delaware was full of budding mediums, and I was not alone. It had been a few months since I had worked at any spa. The solitude of my home and seeing clients from my basement office became a safe harbor for me while I dealt with the shift.

The following story is one of the letters I received from a client I worked with.

***

The first time I met Kathy, I had gone for a spa day. She was very professional and had a very warm and welcoming personality. Time went by, and I wanted to schedule another appointment. She happened to be shopping in the store where I worked, and I mentioned I was going to schedule another appointment. When I finally got around to making the appointment, she was no longer at the salon, so it was a surprise to me when I got there, and it wasn't her. Our paths were meant to cross again, and she came to my store again, this time, we exchanged information, and I scheduled an appointment. She works out of her home, and funny as it maybe, she lives in the neighborhood where I grew up! The day I arrived for my appointment, she said her dog had been acting strange. He never barks, but he had been barking at nothing starting about half an hour before I had arrived. We went down to her salon, and during the massage, I asked her if she and her husband had still been house hunting. She told me about a house they had gone to see but that she wasn't too sure about it, but it gave her an uneasy feeling. Somehow, in the conversation about that house, I asked her if she had ever watched Long Island Medium with Theresa Caputo. She said it was funny I should ask because she has similar capabilities and that she had a feeling that there was someone there waiting for me that day. She asked me if I believe in mediums, and I absolutely do. I always have. I, myself, had never been to one or had an experience before but I do believe. During my massage, she went on to tell me that there was a child energy present. That the child was very excited and happy and wanted to thank me for the way that I honor and remember them. It was so crazy because that next weekend, I was going away, and I had been thinking that it had been a while since I had gone to the grave to pay respects to my cousin, who passed when he was an infant. I never met him. I was a baby myself when he was born, but I have always felt a connection to him and have always wondered how things would have been if he and I had grown up together. No one in my family knows that I would, from time to time, go visit him, so there was no way that Kathy could have or would have known. Kathy said *that there was someone else present but that they weren't too sure yet about the situation. She described the man she saw sitting in the corner of the room, and I knew 100% right away that it was my dad. She finished with the massage and started with my facial. As she proceeded, my dad came through and told me that he knew I was struggling with some tough decisions. That no matter what, he will always love me, and I will always be his little girl. All he wants is for me to be happy. He doesn't want me to settle and make the same mistakes that he made. As Kathy was saying these words to me, I lay there crying. It was the most unbelievable experience I have ever had. These words from my father meant so much for me to hear. Decisions and choices I made before he passed were holding me down. I was afraid to move on with my life because I was afraid that if I made the changes I knew I needed to make I would have tarnished the relationship I had always had with my dad. Something I could never fix and never get back. Knowing that he is with me and knowing that those choices aren't important to him now. Knowing that all he wants for me is for me to be happy has brought me so much peace. It has taken such a load off my shoulders. It was like I could breathe again. I just hope that Kathy knows what a gift she gave me that day. I will be forever thankful. A funny thing, too... after that, I could explain why her dog was barking... my dad was always at least half an hour early for everything.*

***

In September, I signed up to take my first Reiki class at the Pike Creek Reiki Center with Tammy Petrucelli. Reiki is known as Universal Energy Healing, involving a series of hand placements over the seven major chakras as well as the minor chakras located in each joint. The seven major chakras are the Root, Sacral, Solar Plexus, Heart, Throat, Third Eye, and Crown.

I will go into further detail about the chakras in the forthcoming workbook.

The first part of being attuned to Reiki is to heal yourself. Once your attunement begins, your body undergoes a 21-day cleanse, healing body, mind, and soul. After the class, I was assigned to work with 20 people to practice the routines. In early October, I met a man referred to as "Mark Healer Dude," a Reiki Master by night and a professional teacher by day. I was seeking someone to trade energy sessions with, and he offered to exchange with me. During his session, his son, who had passed at birth, entered. He was surprised to find out I was a Medium, Massage Therapist, and Esthetician, and he asked if I would do a trade for our spouses. He would give Conrad his Reiki One attunement in exchange for me giving his wife a day of pampering. I eagerly agreed and asked Conrad if he wanted to participate. The session was scheduled for the following week, and I received the session when Conrad practiced. During that session, I was in a heavenly state, talking with Amy, my neighbor who had committed suicide in 1999. I asked her why I couldn't stay with her, why I had to be here. She told me that I had a lot of work to do on Earth. I went to bed that night, wondering what more I needed to give.

In early November, I was washing dishes at the sink and looking out at the pool. I had a nagging feeling I should check the latch on the pool cover. I went out and adjusted the lock, which appeared to be in place, and then left for lunch at my mom's house. While I was gone, the wind picked up. When I returned home, I thought I should latch the hot tub cover. Going out to the backyard, I saw the pool cover had unraveled and floated to the bottom. I looked up to the sky and said, "Okay, you win." A strange feeling came over me, and I knew my house was no longer mine.

Over the next week, the pool was dismantled in my backyard. I was devastated, as I loved swimming and being out there. Now, my yard and what I loved about it were gone. Unable to bring myself to go outside, I bunkered down in the house. I took it as a sign from the Universe that perhaps my dreams would come true and that I would need to sell my house in time. I began working on my long-term goals for my B&B and imagining what my future would look like.

By early November, I had distanced myself from the group I was training with and sought out other teachers. I joined the local chamber of commerce and began advertising myself as a medium at local business events. We discovered The Center for Joyful Living in Wilmington, a much smaller and diverse church offering a variety of classes. Services began with meditation, often featuring gifted artists playing music from Tibetan singing bowls and wind instruments. I felt very at home there. Many times, they hosted Shamans, Music Healers, and diverse speakers discussing their views on the creator.

In late fall, I woke early one morning from a dream. My son's garage had been broken into, and tools were stolen. It was 3:33 a.m. when I looked at the clock. Just as I was about to go back to bed, I heard my dad's computer start up. I jumped up and told Conrad, "Did you hear that?" Knowing I needed to check on my son's house, I drove over and found everything in order. When I returned, Conrad was waiting for me at the front door.

We went through the holiday season with our new church, which was very different from our past experiences. As New Year's Eve approached, there was a worldwide meditation for peace. To synchronize with others around the world, we were to arrive around 6 a.m. with breakfast to share after the service. On this day, an artist named David Young, who has the amazing ability to play two flutes at the same time, performed. His music was captivating, and his small jokes made it easy to be fixated on him.

At the end of the service, he played John Lennon's "Imagine" and then went around hugging everyone in the room. Never had I experienced such a hug—a hug that felt like being in the clouds. It was different from any hug I had received from parents or husbands; it was akin to holding a newborn baby but with stronger intentions. It felt like all the love in the world came down in that embrace. I turned to Conrad and said, "You have to hug this guy. It's like hugging heaven."

As the sanctuary was rearranged into dining tables, we all assembled where we felt drawn. I was in a small group that included David. I shared my experiences of Moses appearing to me and other events. I knew David was like me—a person connected to spirit and hearing messages. It was a relief to find someone like myself to relate to, someone who had been traveling the world. His fiancée joined, and we all started talking. He took us to his car, which was filled with his music and a book he had written called Channeling Harrison. We followed them to their home, where he gave me CDs of his relaxation music. We felt an instant bond with them and exchanged numbers. In my hands were his book and about five of his CDs, including one I recognized instantly: Mystical Journey. I used that album while working at the Harmony Wellness Center & Spa.

Once home, I sat down with the book and couldn't put it down. Here was someone else experiencing the same things as I was, not a larger-than-life character but someone real. As I read chapter after chapter, his experiences seemed to parallel my own life. Over the past year, I have been receiving references to Eric Clapton's son Conor, who had died. Hearing the song "Tears In

Heaven" made me wonder. One day, while giving Conrad a Reiki session, my iPod malfunctioned, so I switched to my CD player. Then, the iPod unexpectedly switched back on, displaying a picture of a little boy standing in the water—a child who reminded me of an older Conor Clapton. I took a screenshot for later reference and finished the session. I pondered why I was getting information about this child and what it meant.

As I continued reading David's book, his associations with the Beatles and Layla's relationship with Eric Clapton became clearer. A few months earlier, my daughter had brought home a miniature pinscher named Lyla, drawing another connection.

Being a psychic medium was something I had known about myself for a long time, since a very early age. Growing up in an era where such things were not discussed, you can imagine my excitement when John Edward's show aired on TV. I was mesmerized. Most knew me as an intuitive massage therapist, which is how I billed myself. It took several months to fully understand and embrace who I was. I had my dream of a B&B and Spa, and now I had to deal with the reality of being a medium. It gnawed at me, but I kept dreaming of my retreat.

I discussed my dilemma with my therapist, Tanya, as I tried to navigate my new life. I had signed up to be a vendor at Cecil Community College for the January Mind Body Spirit Festival. It had been a year since my father passed away, and as the anniversary approached, I faced my first major event doing readings.

Across from my booth was a vendor named "Angel Chatter," who had an array of products from candles to mists. Something about her intrigued me, and I desperately wanted a reading from her. I went over and scheduled a session. As the reading began, she looked at me and said, "You have big plans? I see a red mill and lots of water around you. Are you planning to live in a hotel or something?"

I blurted out that I wanted to own a B&B. She advised me to create a vision board and include everything I desired.

Conrad and I went to Kmart that night and bought several magazines. I glued pictures of my dream house and all the amenities I wanted onto two giant poster boards, which we pinned to our bedroom wall. Every night, we went to bed staring at these images: the number of rooms, the pictures of lakes, the black Range Rover, and the little benches scattered around the property. Pictures of retail products and fluffy comforters were glued haphazardly around the white paper. I wrote new moon checks in large amounts and glued them to the board. I continued working diligently on my dream of owning a B&B.

On the night of January 12, Conrad and I attended a business mixer at a local restaurant. As we mingled, I came across a man I had met a few months earlier. He had joked about me telling him a story, and I hadn't felt like it at the time. Recently, I had just told my mentor that her class wasn't right for me, and our parting didn't go well. I should have stayed home that night but had promised a client from the chamber that I would accompany her. Here I was, face to face again with this young man who prepares teenagers for college.

I told him I owed him a story and proceeded to share the tale of Conrad's Aunt Anne with the footprints in the sand. When I asked why he had asked me about a message, he revealed that he and his wife had lost a child a few years earlier. I immediately felt like a jerk. Wanting to make up for my previous rudeness, I handed him my card and offered his wife a free massage.

Medium

As the prizes were given out, I gasped when I saw a barefoot bottle of wine with pink feet. It made its way to the young man's arms. From my angle, it was as if his little girl was saying, "Hi Daddy!"

Four nights later, on January 15, I was on my way home from a couple's massage when I felt a great need to surround myself with protective light. I went to bed as soon as I got home and had a restless night. As dawn broke, I felt my left hand reach out to touch someone standing right next to me. Thinking it was Conrad, I then felt someone at my feet. The mattress moved up and down as if someone was trying to wake me. Panicked, I woke up screaming for help. Conrad came in, and I frantically told him what had happened. He tried to calm me before leaving for work.

A few hours later, Conrad called to tell me that Aunt Anne had died during the night. I knew it had to be her at my feet, and the energy to my right felt like Conrad's father. Later that afternoon, as I came home from the store, a barefoot wine cork lay in front of my steps.

Something strange happened at Aunt Anne's funeral at Cathedral Cemetery. We were seated surrounded by caskets, and I looked up to see Steven Jones' casket directly above us. Steven, a police officer, was killed in the line of duty in September 2011. My dad, a retired State Police officer, and I had attended his funeral to pay respects to his wife. My husband works for the same police department Steven served in. A few days after Aunt Anne's funeral, I had a dream where I talked to Steven. He asked, "Didn't you think it was ironic that you sat right in front of my casket?"

I responded, "I thought it was, and I figured you would tell me what it meant." He talked about paying attention to synchronicities and showed me Conrad drying a car, tears in his eyes. We conversed as if this wasn't our first talk but a continuation. The dream ended with children in a bus shaped like an airplane waving at me. Steven seemed like the pilot or bus driver. I waved back from my hiding spot. The scene felt beach-like, and Steven mentioned a sky line that opens sometimes, allowing travel.

On February 5, I had a series of dreams involving someone named Metatron. The dreams happened in three segments, one of which was a conversation with Jaycee. In the dream, she called, asking if she could come over since she didn't have school. When I woke, I recorded these dreams. Later that morning, Jaycee called with the exact message from my dream. Shocked, I looked up Metatron and found out he was an angel who once walked the Earth as a human. I called Conrad, trying to explain my dream and its real-life counterpart. Within hours, Jaycee arrived, and we baked cinnamon rolls as a snowstorm settled in.

Dealing With the Past

Conrad and I signed up to take an advanced Reiki class in Smyrna at the home of Audra Littleton on March 8, 2015. With my phone and my trusty realtor app, we were always on the hunt for potential properties. Once the class finished, we drove to Mud Mill Road and looked at a house that was for sale; it had such potential.

The next morning, after I meditated, I started to write a letter about the Mud Mill house. As I was about to say the phrase, "Do you want me to host," I heard my father's computer sign-on. Hearing it from the hall stopped me dead in my tracks. Once again, my father had gotten my attention.

On March 11, while I was sitting in the driveway of a friend's house, I received a text from my therapist, Tanya, telling me about an essay contest: "How to Win a Country Inn." We constructed our first essay and sent it in.

Later, Conrad and I were gardening, putting pansies into our flowerpots, when I unearthed a large piece of white quartz crystal that appeared to be in the shape of Maine. One of the biggest, most tangible signs we received from that inn was that crystal; it was undeniable that we were headed in the right direction.

Our new friend David Young traveled all over doing sound healing meditations with his music. While sending the essays to the Center Lovell, we were manifesting extra money to cover each submission. David had been in the New England area the week prior and had sold a lot of music. He called from a show in central New Jersey to see if we could deliver him a package of his music. He offered to pay us $100 for the trip.

Within three hours, we were there and stayed for the 90-minute music meditation. The money we needed came in as soon as we asked for it. This was not our regular scheduled money; this was over-the-top money, the kind I had not planned on but urgently needed.

One morning in April, I got a call from Jaycee saying she woke to find her mother not at home. I drove over to her house in New Castle, got her ready for school, and dropped her off. By that afternoon, I received a phone call from a state social worker asking if I would take Jaycee pending an investigation.

In May, we welcomed a new baby into our family, and life took another turn. I envisioned having my grandchildren with me over the summers, just as my Granny Sloan had done with us all those years back.

As the days grew closer to the reveal date, I packed my clothes, gave away items I didn't think I would need, and dreamed of what my new life would look like. The state closed their case with Jaycee's mom, and she went back to New Castle. It seemed like everything was aligning perfectly.

On the morning of the reveal, it became apparent we did not win. My world collapsed; I was confused and did not understand what was happening. How could those signs have been wrong? Many friends contacted us, telling us that something wasn't right and to keep faith that the truth would prevail. My friend Amelia suggested that we still plan our trip as scheduled. We composed ourselves and headed up the long, disappointing drive to Maine. We had no clue what we were going to do or where we were going to go. We grabbed our tents and air mattresses and headed north.

Once in Maine, we drove to Bear Pond, to our family camp, which was now in the hands of someone else. I stopped where the original site of my dream had started and just looked out in utter disbelief. My dreams had come crashing down.

We stayed with my cousins Phil and Dar, who lived just a couple of miles down the road from Bear Pond. We visited with my Aunt Laverna and Uncle Punk, who lived further down Route 219. Then we drove to my Aunt Mate and Uncle Don's house in West Gardner, where we stayed for two more days. Every time I posted on Facebook, my posts would say I was in Purgatory, Maine. As Aunt Mate and I posted on Facebook at the same time on the porch, her account said West Gardner, and my account said Purgatory. I really did not need a Facebook reminder that I was in purgatory; as far as I was concerned, I was in hell.

I had always wanted to see the Finger Lakes, and I asked Conrad to find a place for us to stay at one of them. I did not care where we went, so I said, "Just pick a place." He looked online, found a campground in a state park, booked the cabin, and set the navigator to the new address. We kissed our hosts goodbye and headed south to Ithaca, New York.

On our way there, along the side of the road in New York, we noticed water coming out of the side of a rock wall and a man filling jugs. We decided to pull over and fill our cups with fresh mountain water. I received a message in my head to look up Archangel David. Online, I came across a blog called "The Nature of Being" and read that David is associated with stones and purifying water.

We arrived sometime in the late afternoon at Robert Treman State Park. We found our cabin, unpacked, and began to walk around. I grabbed a few brochures at the desk when we were checking in and discovered that we had landed at Lucifer's Falls. "You have got to be kidding me!" I thought. Within the span of five days, I had felt like I had died, been in purgatory, and now seemed to be in the belly of the beast.

The next morning, Conrad and I decided to walk the entire trail surrounding Lucifer's Falls. Though I was overweight and out of shape, I felt I needed to make this climb. It was the hardest climb I had ever done, but it was beautiful. We hiked to the very top and looked out over the mountain ranges. It was stunning, and most importantly to me, I made it. I didn't have to give up and turn back. I climbed all the way to the top of what seemed to be a devil of a climb.

We walked back down and ended at the waterfalls, a large swimming hole where the water falls into a basin. It was stunning and one of the most beautiful places I have ever been.

I learned so much about myself on that trip. After two days, we returned home to piece together the shattered remnants of my dreams and life. I spent the summer in what appeared to be a slump. My mind needed a break, and I needed to heal.

I enrolled in a soap-making class taught by "Mark Healer Dude" and started making homemade soaps. After two batches, I began to hear that I should start adding stones to my soaps. Confused as to why I would do this, I finally relented and headed to Pike Creek Reiki Center, where I purchased a bag of amethyst stones from Tammy. My first energy soap was made, and I named it Spirit.

One day, towards the end of June, Conrad and I went out to do some shopping. A heavy rain descended upon us as we turned onto Harmony Road, where we saw a couple walking in the rain. I saw a skinny man holding an umbrella over a woman, walking along the shoulder, protecting her from traffic and the rain as best he could. I asked Conrad to pull over and see if they needed a ride. They accepted the offer and, it turned out, were going a half-mile away from where we were headed.

We seemed to talk about everything on that ride, from the churches we were attending to me being a psychic. As we pulled into a shopping center to drop them off, and as we went to say our goodbyes, I felt Corey in spirit come to my left, and someone come down from the right. I heard the words, "This is her divine intervention." The woman, Trina, confessed that she had been battling heroin, which explained Corey. The spirit to my right gave enough information that Trina was confident it was her deceased husband, Mark. She looked over at me and said, "You know, my mom works with a medium up in North Wilmington."

Excitedly, I said, "Is your mom named Tanya?"

She said, "Yes, that's my mom."

"Holy crap! Your mom is my therapist!"

We just sat there, dazed. How could it be that I picked up the child of my therapist? Delaware is small, but it's not that small.

The following Tuesday, when I sat down with my therapist, the first thing she said to me was, "Today's appointment is off the record. I am not charging you for this." She then asked, "How often do you pick strangers up off the highway?"

I just laughed and said, "Not that often." She explained that she had been trying to understand how her daughter ended up in my car. After our third meeting, she thought to herself that if anyone could help her daughter, it would be me. Due to HIPAA laws, she couldn't ethically introduce her daughter to me.

At the time of this encounter, I had been reducing my sessions with Tanya, and we agreed that this would be a good time to conclude. We were both curious about what this all meant, and I wanted to get to know her daughter and see if I could figure out why it all happened the way it did.

My time with Trina has been a rollercoaster of emotions: amazing, sad, worrisome, then elating. I have seen her face defeat as she relapsed and excitement as she rebounded. I will never give up on her because I know she is someone special, and I know we met for a reason that day.

This experience has helped me in ways I couldn't have imagined. Though I am always there to help people in a pinch, it feels like whenever someone is in trouble, I come down like a hot air balloon, landing into their lives with no course or compass to guide me—just floating along toward those who need me.

As summer turned into fall, I attended various mind and body festivals, doing readings and making more soaps. I started working on a line of chakra soaps, spending months perfecting my recipes. As the holiday season approached, we received a phone call informing us that we would have to take Jaycee again. This time, we filed papers to become her guardians soon after Christmas.

In January, we returned to the Elkton Mind Body Festival, and I received a message that it was time to start bottling my massage oils. I looked up the prices of bottles and placed a note to God expressing what I needed. The very next day, a woman came in and bought a massage package, and just like that, the money was there. Conrad spent the winter learning how to make labels, and I began teaching people how to make soap, eventually holding a class at my house.

During the next year, I focused on creating products designed for detox wraps. My sister's interest in cannabis and salves fueled my desire to learn more about the plant. Conrad came up with the name "Foobellas" for my products. Foobella was my childhood nickname, and he thought it was fitting. One day, I researched the name "foo" and discovered that it was what fighter pilots in World War II called the little orbs of light they saw around their planes while in the South Pacific.

A memory came back to me from a meditation session a few years prior. As I lay on the floor listening to the gong, I somehow felt transported back in time. I felt like I was in a tin can and knew I was in the South Pacific. Sarcastically, I thought, "Kathy, how do you know you're in the South Pacific? It's not like there's a road sign that says, 'Greetings, you've just entered the South Pacific, have a safe travel.'" Just then, I looked to my right and saw the tail of a plane with a red moon on it.

At that moment, I thought, "Oh, that's how you know!" I felt the plane get hit, and down we went. As I came out of the meditation, the teacher was holding onto my feet. I couldn't believe what I had just experienced. Was I a gunner on a plane in Hawaii, where my grandfather had served? I was very shaken and didn't know what to think. I felt safe discussing it in that room, but I knew sharing it elsewhere might make me seem crazy.

This experience rattled me, so I decided to read about past lives, including books by Sylvia Browne and Dr. Brian Weiss. Knowing a psychiatrist had written about these experiences in his private practice brought me peace. I eventually decided to undergo a past life regression.

I remember sitting in the chair as my mind began to walk down a hallway with white walls and holes. I knew I was on a boat. Ever since I was young, I've been fascinated by the Titanic. I remember being at a camp in Maine where I either saw a movie or read the book "Raise the Titanic." I talked to Granny about it and told her it would be impossible to raise the boat because it was in two pieces. I recalled walking out the side door of the camp and looking out onto the lake. For a brief second, I saw that boat sitting in the lake. I couldn't have been more than 10 at the time. It was the first time I'd seen anything like that, and I was terrified of what I'd seen and of going into the water. I knew the boat wasn't in that lake, but I had a haunting feeling about all the death lurking beneath the dark water.

One summer, my dad brought up a remote-controlled boat he had built and was playing with it on the water. I recalled being in a smaller boat with him as we tried to retrieve it when the signal went out of range. My dad wanted me to lift the boat out of the water, but all I could do was cry. I was scared to touch the boat because I felt that if I did, all these dead people would rise out of the water, wanting me to save them, and I couldn't do it. I panicked so badly that my dad eventually relented and picked up the small boat himself.

Over the years, I became convinced that I had been on that boat. As I practiced more meditations, I would sometimes feel I was back on it. One night, while Conrad and I were massaging each other, I had an experience that convinced me he was with me. I turned a corner in the meditation, and there he was, standing in a tuxedo. I looked down at myself and saw I was wearing a white, fluffy, apron-type dress, so I knew I was a maid.

For me, this was a culmination of tiny pieces of information slowly dripping in over the years. Seeing him on the boat explained an incident that happened on our honeymoon. I wanted to try to get over my fear of boats and water, so I asked Conrad if we could do a banana boat ride. I was nervous but determined to conquer my fears.

The ride was fun until the boat hit a wave at a hard angle, and we were all catapulted into the water. We were wearing life preservers, and I started swimming toward Conrad. As I approached him, he was in complete panic and frantically tried to climb on top of me in the water. I had to push him off and swim to shore as fast as I could. The water was crystal clear, and as soon as I could touch the bottom, I turned around to check on him. I shouted to see if he could feel the bottom with his feet. Eventually, we both made it to shore. The walk up to the boathouse was very quiet; neither of us mentioned what had happened. We just returned the jackets and pretended nothing had happened.

A few weeks after we got home, something similar happened with him and my son in my sister's pool. They were all horsing around when suddenly Conrad climbed up my middle son in a panic. My oldest son had to wrestle him off his brother. It was very unsettling, and we didn't know what to do. Conrad apologized immediately, and we all went into family counseling.

It took years to piece together why he panics so badly in the water. Once we did, we realized that these were memories from his past life, and he was recalling the panic of his death.

One day, during a meditation, I experienced what felt like a death spiral. I felt myself falling and my body going in different directions. I remembered hitting the water and going under. When my body rose to the surface, I felt alive. In the meditation, I looked up at the propellers. At that moment, I knew instantly where my fears of boats and propellers came from. I pulled myself out of the meditation, not wanting to relive the boat crashing down on me again. I accepted that it had happened and decided to work through my fears of boat motors. Eventually, I touched the propellers on boats in my neighbors' yards.

Reliving this past life explained so much about my unrealistic fears of boats and planes. When we went to the Dominican Republic, it was my first time on a plane. We chose that destination so I could get over my fear of flying.

I spent much of the last year exploring my past to overcome the things I feared most in this life. One such fear involved a memory that surfaced during my meditations related to that boat. I knew I had been prostituting myself to the people on that boat. I believe I was an Irish immigrant searching for a better life in America. I knew Conrad was a man I was with at that time. I don't believe we died together; I have yet to see any memory of that, but I do believe we knew each other on that boat.

Who I Am

I have always found it difficult to reconcile my roles as a massage therapist and a wife. Incorporating massage techniques into our lovemaking has perplexed me for years, and it took my entire career to untangle these thoughts. What I learned is that I am a sexual being called to a healing profession.

The realization struck me as I walked up the steps to my home after a lunch date with my son. I felt a presence pass by and recognized the blue sweater—it was my dad's mother, Rosemary, who had passed away years before. The memories overwhelmed me, taking me back in time. Struggling to control the situation, I decided to take a relaxing bath.

I filled the tub with a mineral soak called "Spirit," which I created myself, and tried to calm my mind. Suddenly, I was transported back to when I was about eight years old, visiting my dad's parents in the mountains of Pennsylvania. I remember being sent into a dark room with a young man watching television. My only memory of him was eating a banana with mayonnaise and offering it to me. At that moment in the tub, I realized the banana was not a banana, and the mayonnaise was not mayonnaise.

What happened next is a blur, and it's better that way. I understood the meaning of what occurred and why. I found answers to lifelong questions: Why didn't I enjoy sex? Why did I feel it was wrong? Why didn't I feel worthy? I believe my grandparents walked in on a crude game of Spin the Bottle rather than an actual act of sex. I felt relieved to finally understand this confusing memory.

This marked the beginning of my journey toward sexual healing—from those to whom I gave my body to those I wanted but did not. It was a conscious release, done as I was ready to let go. By reevaluating past experiences and choosing different paths mentally, I saw the energies of loss, regret, and blame vanish. As I breathed through these moments, I understood why I needed these experiences to help others release what no longer serves them.

Carrying judgmental memories is heavy baggage, manifesting physically. My goal is to help release that energy. It's a slow process; just as it took time to bury these issues deeply, it takes time to surface them. Some healers refer to these issues as "demons," but I prefer "memories that no longer serve their highest purpose." Being chosen to aid in someone's healing is an immense honor and responsibility. Healing on an energetic level requires a significant decision and leap of faith, opening my eyes to solutions that weren't previously obvious.

Desperate for help, I chose to work with an energy healer and cannabis as a healing plant, having exhausted all modern conventions. I have been blessed to learn the difference and fortunate to hear clients' stories of healing. Their triumphs are interwoven with mine, forming a shared tapestry of the universe. I love doing the healing work, listening to spirits' guidance, and following their instructions during sessions.

I was taught to believe sex was bad and bombarded with images and messages enforcing this belief. As I healed internally, I recognized the need for significant sexual healing. Over 18 months, I experienced a range of transformative events, providing a blueprint for my healing and aiding others.

In early October 2015, we camped at Killen's Pond near the Apple Scrapple Festival. That rainy night, an image of an Indian man approached me in my mind's eye. Guides instructed me to breathe deeply and follow their directions, leading to a transformative experience of brilliant white light flowing through my spine. This allowed me to experience whole-body releases and guide others similarly.

Conrad and I explored sensual massage techniques, and I realized I could no longer work on men. I love massaging, feeling the body's curves, and embracing the sensual side I had buried for years. Releasing this part of myself was inevitable.

I've observed that massage serves different purposes: pain relief, human touch, or sensual connection. Touch is vital for many people's health and happiness, though some can live without it. For many, massage fills that void.

Unfortunately, human trafficking masquerades as massage, exploiting innocent girls under false promises. This has led to more regulations for licensed professionals to prevent illicit behavior. My biggest challenge was incorporating sex into massage as our needs as a couple evolved. My views on massage, marijuana, and their applications were being reshaped, challenging long-held beliefs.

I had tried smoking pot when I was younger and never felt that I got much from it. I didn't like anything in my lungs. One day, a friend gave me a pot-laced brownie. I decided to try it, thinking it wouldn't affect me. I had a massage scheduled with a long-time client when I began to feel its effects. Never in my life did I enjoy giving a massage as much as I did that day. I felt like my whole heart was open, and I enjoyed just massaging her. It felt like all my cares and worries were out the door, and for that span of time, I could just be in the moment.

It was what began to happen that night with Conrad that caught my attention. My body seemed to open to him in a way I had never felt before. I was relaxed and started to enjoy the experience way more than I ever did. Excited by this newfound sex tool, I began to consider trying it again. I worked up the nerve to try another product, just to see what my body would do.

What I have learned about cannabis is that it is a gateway to healing. It opens the door in meditation to regions that would otherwise take years of intense work to achieve. I had a lot of learning to do, many amends to make, and numerous perceptions to change in my head.

One of the most amazing women I ever encountered was my Aunt Debbie. From the time I was little, I could be her pain in the ass or her best friend. Aunt Debbie was the fifth child of my grandparents and was eleven years older than me. Her blue eyes and red hair made her personality stand out even more. Her love of rock and roll was evident, with songs by Led Zeppelin and Rod Stewart always playing. The song that spoke to me the most about her was "Free Bird" by Lynyrd Skynyrd. She was the poster child for sex, drugs, and rock and roll. Often, my granny would send me to her room to look for her stash of pot. I usually found it hidden in record albums and promptly delivered the bag of goods to my granny. We would take the secret stash and flush it down the toilet.

As time went by, Aunt Debbie settled into married life and started having babies. Mom and Debbie were pregnant at the same time with Amanda and my cousin. Later, Debbie and I were both pregnant at the same time. Life seemed to come full circle and this time I developed a different relationship with her. She was now my friend. Our kids would play together, and we would have coffee almost every morning while they did. I loved her more than life itself, and she was my best friend, someone I misunderstood on so many levels.

She would tell me stories of walking me around the block, getting me to smell flowers, and encouraging me to say "bullshit" at all the wrong times just to embarrass Granny. We would go on secret sleuth missions where I would cash checks from her husband's business account so she could buy groceries. I always had special instructions that allowed for some extra cash.

My Aunt Debbie died on January 3, 2009. Her loss was devastating to me. She was my morning coffee person, and I miss her greatly.

That summer, our family went to the camp in Maine, which was now in the hands of my Aunt Mate. An orange butterfly had been flying around all of us and landing on the kids. I kept saying it was Aunt Debbie, and we took pictures. Each time I saw an orange butterfly, I would say, "Hi, Aunt Debbie," and take a picture.

In late February, I was contacted to do a reading for Della, a friend from Kmart, and her neighbor. As the first reading started, I began to see a cop I was familiar with, then a cop who was ambushed in Philadelphia at the shipyard. I saw a state police officer with blonde hair who was killed on Route 13. I thought, "Wow, there are a lot of cops here," and then I realized, "Oh, you're a cop." This turned out to be the foundation for something else.

My second reading was for Della. She emigrated from Germany, and her thick accent required careful listening to understand her. Her husband came through loud and clear, bobbing in the water. He had been buried at sea, and his urn refused to sink for the longest time. As her reading continued, he kept telling me to pull my pendulum out of my purse. He kept referring to her upcoming surgery and begged her to look at alternatives. I pulled out my pendulum, which pointed directly to the part of her shoulder with the issue. X-rays confirmed what her problem was. She reassured me that she had tried all types of therapy and that surgery was her only choice.

Conrad and I were working to complete the required practice sessions for our Reiki 2 attunements, and we asked if Della would help Conrad reach his goal of 20 practice sessions. She happily agreed and came over a few days later. Conrad and I did the session together, and it was a highly active healing. Then she began belching deeply, releasing something from within her stomach. Embarrassed, we reassured her it was normal and not to worry.

Over time, as I did more readings and built up my stamina, my information started to come in differently. Once I mastered the way the information was coming in, I found I would level up. Eventually, I engaged more in the conversation, learning to trust my information and ask my guides questions in my mind. Initially, I had a spirits visit during my clients' massages, facials, and Reiki sessions. I had to learn to turn it on and off. That was difficult because it crept up on me so slowly that I didn't realize I was on all the time.

One morning, I had an 8 a.m. facial. The woman, whom I will refer to as Mrs. "P," said to me, "Kathy, something just happened. As you were massaging my hand, I felt your hand change. As it got bigger, I thought, 'That feels like my husband Joe holding my hand.'" I know her late husband reached through me to hold his wife's hand one more time. To witness that kind of love and be the bridge connecting someone like that is one of the best parts of this job. I love how this can come into my massages. I have always felt that massage is for healing the body, and messages from the spirit can also heal. Delivering both at the same time brings me much peace.

In August, Conrad and I headed to Pot Nets for the weekend. Frustrated that our dreams of a B&B weren't happening, we began to consider different options. Maybe we should just retire in a place like Pot Nets, get a few crab pots, and enjoy retirement life.

We talked the whole way home, and I said, "Okay if this is the route, I need a sign from the Universe to either give up on my dreams or go forward." Within a few minutes, we received a call from Della. We put it on speaker so we could both listen and what she said changed our minds. She told us that the night after her session, her belching stopped, and the pain in her arm went away. She woke up the next day, and it was still gone. She decided to proceed with the surgery, but when they opened her up, there was nothing to fix. All the calcification seen in earlier X-rays was gone. The doctors were baffled, trying to figure out how her body had healed. They sewed her back up and suggested physical therapy. After two appointments, she was discharged. When a friend from Germany visited, she told them about her miraculous healing, and her friend encouraged her to call us and share her story.

I continued my training with a local shaman. The time it took to build just my chakra line was staggering, not to mention learning how to market my products. We prepared for our first open house featuring Foobellas products on Small Business Saturday. It turned out to be our best show yet, and we didn't have to transport a single item. As the day ended and we assessed our success, we knew it had been an overwhelming triumph. We packed the remaining items in preparation for our next show in Canton, Massachusetts, on December 10, 2016.

As we approached the venue, we saw we were the first to arrive. We drove off to find some coffee before heading back, only to see another couple arrive and begin unloading their wares. Another car pulled up next to us, and we rolled the windows down to start a conversation with a woman who introduced herself as Kelly Stack. She makes jewelry and travels all over the New England area.

Kelly turned out to be our angel that day, and she said something that immediately caught my attention. She asked where we were from, and I said Delaware, explaining that this was our leap of faith. Kelly told me that early in her travels, she had taken a leap of faith by going to a show in Maine. When I asked her what part of Maine, she responded with Turner, I gasped and said, "You wouldn't believe me if I told you, but my dream is to have a healing center on the lake in the town right above it called North Turner."

Later, Kelly told me she would never forget that place because it was in a building with an odd name. When she mentioned it was the Boofy Quimby Memorial Hall, I was stunned. With extreme excitement, I told her, "That wasn't Turner, Maine; you were in North Turner, Maine! The home of my future retreat center!"

Once again, my attention had shifted to Maine.

White Christmas

January 5, 2017, started like any other day. Around noon, I felt a strange sensation that compelled me to lie down and take a nap. I later discovered that this was the exact moment the New Castle County Drug Enforcement Unit was raiding my sister Jessica's house. Jessica had been a prominent activist for the legalization of cannabis. During that raid, my Uncle Russell was arrested and charged with drug trafficking. I asked him to stay at our house while everything got sorted out, picked him up, and brought his clothes to our home.

Meanwhile, my daughter and her boyfriend were traveling from Dover to Philadelphia to meet his family for Christmas dinner. I had a massage scheduled for noon, and as I was getting ready, my daughter called me to say that their car had broken down in Odessa and asked if Conrad could come to get them. I was occupied with a client, but Conrad immediately sprang into action and left to help with the car.

After my client left, my daughter called again to inform me that the motor mount had broken and the engine was on the ground. They asked if they could use the truck to continue their journey to Philadelphia, and we agreed. However, the snowfall intensified, making it unlikely they would make it to Philly. Later, another call came through, saying the car had been temporarily fixed and they were on their way to our house.

I had a large bag of chicken breasts and initially planned to portion the ten pounds of chicken to make several meals throughout the week. As I was dredging and frying the chicken, I decided, "Screw it. I'm just going to make a big tray of roasted chicken." Then, I received another call: the car broke down again, this time in front of Delmarva Power, a few miles from our home. While cleaning up from my preparations, I got a text from my daughter that read, "Mom, his family is coming to our house. Clean the toilets!" According to her, she asked more sweetly, "Tell Kathy we're coming to her house."

I was prepared, and in less than an hour, 13 people were gathered around our table. Within two hours, they were in our living room. During that last hour, I handed our guests a bar of our "World Peace" soap and welcomed his family into our home. Conrad drummed as I led everyone in Meditation.

The thing I remember most about that night is the snow. It was our first White Christmas. As the snow continued to fall, so did the pieces of life. As the days unfolded, I realized that the universe had provided everything I needed. I had the food prepared; my Uncle Russell ran around the house helping me clean and set the table. This was our first sign of what was to come. Exactly three weeks later, we posted an invitation to dinner and healing on Facebook, and about ten people came. The following week, we did the same and had another amazing night. And so, it was born. I changed the name of my business to Kathy's House of Healing.

Rebirth

On February 1, 2017, I had a dream where I was drowning. I could feel death, but it didn't feel like I was dying; instead, it felt like I was with God, preparing to explore a new realm. I was floating in the ocean, and all I can remember was a profound sense of peace. Strangely enough, I also recall feeling myself submerged under the water. I knew I was being held down, but I didn't experience any fear; I didn't think I was dying. It felt like I was about to enter Heaven, and I was incredibly excited. I couldn't wait to pass through the opening ahead of me. I saw a clearing, seemingly lined with a fluffy, golden mist. I knew I was flailing my arms, trying to swim toward that bright light. An energy was drawing me in, and I wanted to be in it so badly.

Just then, our cat Wednesday scratched at the door, and I woke up from the dream. My first thought was, "Oh no! I was almost there!" Once I was fully awake, I began to feel fear as it settled in that I had felt death. I woke Conrad up and asked him to hold me while I recounted the dream. That day also happened to be my birthday. I remember talking with Conrad, wondering if the dream had any significance; why would I dream about death on my birthday?

I finally got out of bed to the sound of Jaycee making me a birthday breakfast. I opened a card from my mother, which she had dropped off the night before. Inside was enough money for me to treat myself to a pedicure. I decided to try a different place than usual. There, the nail technician spoke to me in a way I understood as a message being delivered. I was told that I needed to cast a larger net. Over the years, I was told I would write a book. Never did I think I was qualified to write one. The determination to undertake such a large project wasn't something I felt I had within me, but I knew I was running out of time. I spent the afternoon in meditation, and these are the words that came to me.

***

This is me now. This is the raw you. You are talented beyond what we expected of you. We are immensely proud of your accomplishments. I trust you, The Universe, I trust you The Universe, I trust you The Universe. Take a deep breath. Bring that in. Bring that in deep. Take a deep breath. Feel your heart jump; feel it start like an engine roaring toward destiny. I am triumph, I am beauty, I am confident, I love fiercely loved, I am honest, I am loved, I am love, I am I.

***

Throughout the month of February, I began writing down my story. The more I wrote, the more I seemed to unravel. Conrad had been complaining of shoulder pain for a few months, and it seemed to be getting worse each day. Whenever I suggested he see a doctor, it became a battle of wills between us.

On the night of February 26, Conrad mentioned that he was experiencing chest and arm pain again. I tried to persuade him to let me call an ambulance or at least take him to the hospital. We argued back and forth until he suddenly demanded that I heal him. Enraged by his tone and refusal to seek help, I snapped back, "I can't help you!"

He lay in bed complaining throughout the night and awoke the next morning still in pain and upset. He headed to work regardless. I was having lunch with a women's group when Conrad called me: "I'm in the ambulance headed to Christiana Hospital with chest pains." I was only a minute away and arrived before he did. His EKG looked normal, and I kept questioning if they were sure it wasn't a "widow-maker" heart attack. The nurse reassured us that such an issue would show up on the EKG, suggesting something else was the problem. When he had been in the hospital about a year earlier with the same symptoms, we were told it was his pancreas, but all subsequent tests outside the hospital disproved that theory. This time, they called in his heart doctor, and the doctors confidently attributed his pain to acid reflux, prescribing him Nexium.

I was beginning to unravel. I pressured the doctors to conduct more tests and questioned them again about the widow-maker. Frustrated and realizing they weren't listening to me, I decided to change my approach.

When the nurse arrived, I told her that Conrad was just having panic attacks and worrying about finances and other issues. I even wagered that I was right. The nurse, clearly angered, informed me of her many years of training. I crossed my arms over my chest and said, "Prove me wrong." A few minutes later, a doctor asked Conrad if he could trigger the pain by walking the hall. Conrad replied, "I can't guarantee it." Shortly after, the nurse informed us they would perform a stress test, then moments later changed their mind and admitted him for further tests. A PET dye test revealed that he had blockages. The doctors scheduled him to have stents put in the next day, but an emergency delayed the procedure until the following morning.

I went to the hospital that night with a deck of cards to play Rummy, a game we turned to during snowstorms or tight financial times. The following morning, I watched the board displaying patient identification numbers to track his room. After a few hours, the doctor approached me and informed me that Conrad had over 90 to 95 percent blockages in four arteries going to his heart and that two stents had been placed. My jaw dropped.

Reflecting on my behavior that day in the hospital, I realized I was struggling to reconcile my instincts with the machine's data.

Conrad came home to recover, and we began a long healing process. We engaged in every healing activity I could think of and increased our sexual energy healing sessions. It became clear how close I had come to losing my husband, and I vowed to do everything to save him. We had warning signs, like erectile dysfunction, which indicated that blood was not flowing properly throughout his body. I began paying closer attention to our health.

We immersed ourselves in metaphysical books and began adopting more positive thoughts into our daily lives. We continued to host healing nights, inviting anyone who wanted to join us. One night, I was instructed to prepare towels in my large cooking roaster, filling it with crystals and my anointing soap. Jessica and other local healers joined us, and together, we washed everyone's feet. The energy in the room was powerful, and as people shared their experiences, it was clear they felt profoundly touched.

We hosted another dining event with an open invitation. Our doors opened at 6 p.m., and we served whatever was on the table, followed by drumming and meditations. Each event has been amazing, and I believe those who come are meant to be there. Feeling nostalgic, I cooked a dinner that my Grandmother Sloan used to make at the camp. When it rained, she would make a casserole. After a nasty ice storm, I decided her California chicken would be good comfort food. It was what our guests brought that delivered a message to me. Weeks earlier, we had posted our "Dinner & Meditation" event on Facebook. A woman named Alayna commented that she couldn't make it that night but would love to come another time.

When she was able to attend, Alayna messaged me to confirm and asked if she could bring dessert for her 18-month-old toddler. I agreed, and what transpired was magical. Alayna brought a very special dessert: ambrosia, an old church recipe made of canned fruit cocktails, coconut flakes, Jell-O, and Cool Whip. My granny used to make it every Easter, although Alayna called it something else. Now, this old favorite has a new name: "Better Than Sex on the Beach." My uncle and I realized it was Granny Sloan making her presence known.

My Granny Sloan had many talents, one of which was painting. As a graduation gift, she gave me a painting of tulips, which now hangs on the wall in my home. My house is filled with furniture and objects from deceased relatives, from the cast-iron shoes of my father's grandfather to the antique tables of my mom's grandparents. My yard is filled with flowers from more deceased people's yards than I can count. When the figs emerge, I think of my grandmother Andreavich, and when the purple irises bloom, I remember my Grandmother Sloan and Maine. I took those purple irises from the camp property before my aunt sold it, and they thrive beside my hot tub.

These things—the flowers, the painting, the furniture—have somehow shaped who I am. However, painting was something I never thought I was destined to do. Over the past three years, I have felt called to create numerous paintings. The very first one came after a profound session when I had my initial experience with a higher energy source.

I woke up in the middle of the night with a sensation that the top of my head was being unscrewed, producing a sound reminiscent of clay jars. In my confusion, I asked, "Jesus, is this You?"

The reply came, "No."

I then took a deep breath and asked, "God?" Suddenly, a bright light shot into the top of my head and traveled all the way down my spine. It felt as if beams of light were radiating from my spinal joints, causing my entire body to shake as if I were convulsing. It felt incredible as if the whole bed was vibrating.

From that moment, I knew I needed to paint. I purchased a small canvas and the colors that resonated with me. Searching my basement, I found a bucket of joint compound. I scooped the compound into several bowls and mixed in the different paints. I then invited my artist friend Tricia to view my work. She took one look and said, "You need to go bigger." Go bigger? I could barely manage what I had.

That night, Conrad took me to an art supply store. As we approached the supplies, a lone canvas lay on the floor. Conrad said, "That's the one." Intimidated by its size, I searched for something smaller.

Yet, Conrad stood back and insisted that the right one was already waiting for me. "Just take it, and let's go." Reluctantly, I picked up what felt like a massive canvas and brought it home.

The next morning, I laid the canvas on my kitchen table and filled the bowls with joint compound and paint. Closing my eyes, I used my hands to massage the mixture into the fabric, employing various massage techniques like gliding strokes, tapotements, and effleurage. As the paint dried, I felt something was missing. On my kitchen windowsill stood a small bottle of pearl glitter my father had bought for an unfinished project. When we cleaned out his belongings, this bottle was left behind. I dusted the pearl flakes over the wet canvas. In the end, the painting evoked many things for me. I saw the Universe, an angel, and the pearly dust as all the souls of the universe. I named this painting "Being With The Universe."

My second painting hangs in our bedroom. It was a homework assignment from my therapist, meant to convey my feelings. I painted a large sky filled with clouds, reminiscent of those from my childhood summers in Maine with my grandparents at 21 Beach Street, North Turner. Behind the house was a giant ditch that turned into a mud bath when it rained. I would roll in the mud, gaze up at the sky in wonder, and after the sun dried the mud on my skin, I would run to the lake to wash it off. This is where I envisioned my retreat center on Bear Pond, combining my passion for helping couples heal with the joys of summer.

The sun in my painting sits amidst the clouds, its rays filled with vibrant colors representing my swirling ideas and thoughts. These colors symbolize everything I am creating—soaps, massage oils, books, massages, food, and concepts. The sun's rays form a vortex of my creativity. Hands appear beside the sun, positioned to receive all that I am willing to create and manifest. I call this painting "Gazing at the Sun."

It's no surprise that I developed a Chakra line of products. Each Chakra is represented by a color, featured in soaps and massage oils adorned with stones. The first soap I made was called Spirit, using oils I had bathed in the night my father died, which I regard as my coming-out party. From there, I created the Root, Sacral, Solar Plexus, Heart, Throat, and Crown blends. Some blends have been in use for years, while others have taken significant effort to develop. The Throat blend was the last to be created and required substantial work for me to release my truth to the world.

We were inspired to create another soap titled "World Peace," which I gave as gifts to my family. It is a blend of female and male energy, made with figs from our backyard tree, sage, lemon, and lavender, and infused with either rose quartz or hematite charged under a full moon. Like all our soaps, these were attuned and blessed.

I also make four types of deodorants, five different blends of body scrubs and lip balms, and over twelve different types of massage oils, including the Chakra line and a muscle and relaxation blend.

Do Not Be Afraid

I have learned so much about how cannabis can help people, and as a massage therapist with 20 years of experience in healing, I can no longer stay silent. I can no longer watch my own children suffer and do nothing. I can no longer look at my husband and worry that he will share the same fate as his father or mine. I can no longer ignore the evidence. It is time to make things right. It is time for the truth to come out and for us to start healing the world. The truth is, I would never have realized my own sexual self without consuming a cannabis-infused product. I have been a teacher all my life, and now it's time to teach people what I've learned.

In truth, I will never sell sensual massages to the masses by personally providing the service. What I want to do is teach couples how to perform these massages for each other. What I discovered is that massaging each other has been a wonderful way to enhance our marriage. We have learned to be each other's healers. No one on earth knows us more intimately than we know each other. I adore his foot massages, although he couldn't paint my nails to save his life. I'm not suggesting that anyone replace skilled technicians. What I am saying is that we should do what we can and seek help for what we can't. Everyone has needs, and those needs vary from person to person.

Massage is very sensual because touch feels amazing. Being able to give and receive from your partner is beyond beautiful; it's magical. When you learn how to touch your partner, you can enhance your lovemaking. For years, I kept the two separate out of fear. It took cannabis to allow my mind to relax enough to feel pleasure. Talking to other women and men, I realized I was not alone in my struggles. I discovered I was frustrated beyond belief. I took medication for years that inhibited my ability to achieve orgasm, but just one pot brownie changed my life.

We live in a world that has guilted us for everything. Guilt serves an immense purpose. According to Dictionary.com, guilt is "the fact or state of having committed an offense, crime, violation, or wrong, especially against moral or penal law." There it is: moral or penal law. What you believe determines your guilt. I was taught that if I touched myself, I would go blind. That was the law I was taught. I believed it was wrong because I was programmed to think so. Guilt has been a powerful tool for submission over time.

We saved our marriage by massaging each other, giving body scrubs and mud wraps, and ultimately committing to healing each other with Reiki. I saved myself by learning the truth about cannabis.

***

A large wave comes crashing down

against the rock, splashing and sending a ripple

from your root chakra, all through the top of your head

sending a massive tidal wave of color exploding in you.

***

This is how I integrated the seven chakras into my personal life and healing journey. My seven realizations have prepared me to share them with you. It took a lot of learning, crying, healing, and faith. But in the end, I am confident the work will be worth it.

The Root Goal

Knowing exactly who I am and acknowledging that my story has shaped me into the person I am today. I am a ball of energy, and in human form, I am surrounded by bone and soft tissue that can hold and release energy as I choose. Everything I feel, taste, see, and touch, including what I carry from past lives, is part of me. It has taken me my entire life to discover my true self. I must understand that I am my number-one priority, and I must fulfill my own needs first. Only when my cup is full can I give to others. I deserve to take care of my needs and wants first. By taking care of myself, I can then care for others. When I give thanks for the experiences in my life and dive deep into my own challenges, only then will I truly see myself. It is easy to see flaws in others but difficult to see them in ourselves. Accepting this truth allows us to ask in any situation, "Why did this situation present itself to me? What can I learn?" We must examine ourselves within.

Let me give you an example. I had an opportunity to go on a ride with a friend who was under a time crunch. Ten minutes from our goal, a phone call resulted in a 20-minute diversion. The goal wasn't achieved, and my friend was 45 minutes late for her appointment. I realized that I attracted this lesson by focusing my attention. It became clear why I hadn't focused on finishing this book; I let myself be distracted. I could have been angry, but I chose to thank and forgive that person for the adventure. After meditating and journaling, I understood my focus: take your time and be gentle with yourself and the process.

The Sacral Goal

Accepting myself as a sexual being involves understanding that my body and its sexual components are magical. As a woman, I have the incredible gift of potential motherhood; as a man, the potential to father a child. This does not mean I will necessarily use this ability, but its presence means the Universe designed this area for incredible pleasure. Feeling guilty about understanding this incredible machine is a disservice to life's process. Many of us have been shamed about our sexual bodies. Our bodies mature, grow hair, and emit hormones, naturally prompting us to reproduce. It is human nature to be physically attracted to others. When we judge someone's reproductive choices, we must examine the truths within ourselves and ask, "Am I still judging myself for my past behaviors?"

An example: As a child, my grandparents walked in on me and a cousin, showing each other our body parts. We were too young to know better. I was scolded and told it was bad. Now, I understand and hold no ill will; my grandmother's intention was to teach me how my body worked. I needed that lesson.

The Solar Plexus Goal

Realizing that I am my own powerhouse means harnessing my energy to create abundance in my life. Using my Universal-given abilities and experiences to better myself and the world and understanding that creating something might take many attempts. Sometimes, my specific creations failed, and I would either scrap or destroy them.

For instance, I made body scrubs that often melted on hot days, ruining the consistency and labels. One day, a test batch of deodorant failed. Initially upset over wasting pricey ingredients, I let the mixture sit. Later, adding salt to it, I discovered it no longer separated and solved my previous scrubs' issues. My perceived error was a breakthrough.

The Heart Goal

Understanding my heart is crucial, as my family has a history of heart disease. My father died after complications from open-heart surgery. My husband, whose father also died of heart disease, eventually required two stents. I needed to heal my own heart. Mourning loss – be it of a person, innocence, or seeing suffering – can block or open the heart. When open, it embraces love and beauty; when closed, it shuts out the world's wonders. Only we can answer how to heal our hearts.

For example, I desired to create a couple's B&B healing retreat inspired by my first failed marriage. Addressing heart issues before reaching critical overload might have bettered our understanding and resolved conflicts. I realized my husband was showing his broken heart, but I learned the lesson too late. My desire now is to help save other couples from similar pain.

The Throat Goal

To speak my truths to the world, aiming to show couples how to connect energetically.

For instance, we tested our theory using pendulums during my husband Conrad's recovery from heart procedures. Full-body releases were abundant, and if we can teach these techniques, we are confident they can restore deeper satisfaction in relationships.

Speaking my truth required putting myself out there, using my life experiences for the greater good, and healing many hearts as a vessel.

The Third Eye Goal

To trust and understand my intuition and the knowledge within me. Believing the information I receive is clear and for the highest good.

For example, this book exists because I trusted my instincts and intuition, using my third eye throughout the writing process.

The Crown Goal

To trust I am never alone and always in unity with the Universe. This is personal due to a misdiagnosis of bipolar disorder years ago. Rather than focus on clinical definitions, I view it spiritually. What if mania connects us to the Universe on the highest levels, depression signifies disconnect, and equilibrium represents normalcy?

An example: During massive projects, I become hyper-focused. I once persuaded 13 churches to host a fundraiser for Family Promise of New Castle County, DE, raising over $6,600. My manic devotion fueled this successful effort, benefiting countless families. Thus, I regard channeling the Universe's glory as a profound, invaluable experience.

And the Truth Shall Set You Free

I remember a high school teacher warning us that if we wore jean jackets and smoked cigarettes, we would be a "sluggo." He would walk right up to my face, bellowing, "You don't want to be a sluggo, do you?" Shaking my head, I muttered a soft "no." I didn't want to be anything that someone would look down upon. I wouldn't even dare look at a guy with a jean jacket for fear our eyes would connect, and I would be labeled a sluggo. We were taught to be prejudiced, all of us; from the moment we are born, we are taught to hate one thing or another. Judging other people seems to come naturally. We judge everything, from the restaurants we like to the clothes we wear. What I've learned is that each situation and person teaches us something, one way or another. You evaluate them to determine if they will help you on your journey. If you decide they won't, you move on.

I knew that writing this book and teaching people these lessons could lead to judgment. I was told that if I wanted to succeed, I had to stop using a pole and start using a net. We have struggled with marriage; it's not easy, but we have found that the energy sessions we were guided to create saved us, and we need to reach the world to teach couples how to do this. In a perfect world, this is what I would do. However, I have learned that just because it's what I want to do does not mean it's what I am supposed to do.

Early on, when I started doing energy work, I had a young woman on my table who happened to be a linguistics major at Delaware State University. I remember pulling what seemed to be balls of energy out of her, slinging the black muck against the walls, and chanting in a language I subconsciously knew. At that moment, I knew exactly what to do and say, even though I had no pre-thought process when I started. After her session, she said, "Holy shit, you are the real deal." When I asked why, she told me I was speaking Latin and begging God to bring more angels.

Some of my energy sessions were ramped up—or, for lack of a better word, crazy! When these sessions happened, they seemed to take a few days for me to recover. I would feel drained as if I had run a race. What I have realized is that the more issues a person is experiencing in their private life, the more energy comes into the session to help them, and the more it takes from me to get through it.

One night, a young man was in my home and confessed he was having some problems. As he sat in the chair, I asked if I could just put my hands on his heart and his back. I took several deep breaths and felt like I was inside. As my energy traveled further into his body, I felt the knocks from deep within him. It felt like his soul was telling me to get him, and I could hear him banging to get out. I knew I needed to get deeper into his being to do anything significant that night. The magic words came when he asked me to massage his back. I knew then

I had permission to work on him and led him down to my office. I knew this kid struggled with heroin, and I had been wanting to get my hands on him for a long time. I asked him to lie on the floor while I straddled his back. My hands compressed from his lower to upper back, and on the third compression, it felt like a trap door opened. My nails transformed into claws, my legs felt like they turned into hindquarters, and brown hair covered my body. I roared with a voice that felt like my own, as if I were the bear, lashing out at the beast holding this kid's soul captive. My jaws opened wide, roaring in a language only this beast and I understood. Without struggle, I felt myself pulling the child's soul away from the creature, rescuing him from hell. It was over in seconds. The young man, still shaking, walked up the stairs and out the door, unnerved and unaware of what had just occurred.

Had I known, I might not have done it. Had he known, it might have freaked him out more than the addiction itself. From his perspective, he had a woman over him who began howling and roaring while placing her hands on his back. I don't blame him for being scared. I was, too. I'm still scared, especially for all the people battling every day with this beast that has found a home in so many. My Uncle Russell said it sounded like I was doing an exorcism. Jaycee's mom, who was also in the house at the time, said she heard me roaring and speaking in an unknown language.

I had never experienced anything this terrifying in all my work. I tried to explain everything to Conrad, but all I could do was ask him to read the Bible to me. It felt like I needed him to pull me out of the hell I had naively entered. This experience shook me to my core. I had no idea that leading the young man down the steps would result in confronting something so sinister. A friend told me I didn't see anything more than his hell.

I have felt very conflicted since. In my massage therapy career, I always knew that if the problem was in the back, go to the front. There is an up and a down, a left and a right. If I believe the white light protects me, I must believe it is protecting me from something I need protection from. Though nothing would make me happier than to work with couples and help them heal their relationships, I cannot ignore the fact that people addicted to heroin or alcohol keep crossing my path. Corey lost his battle that day, and the fight to help people overcome addiction is real. It is, in my opinion, much more than just a physical addiction; it is a spiritual attack unlike anything I could have ever imagined. When this base plant is cut and reformulated, it is done with the most dangerous substances.

I wish this was made up. I wish that what I've written was some fantasy from my overactive imagination. But it was not. It was something I went through. Many times since I have questioned whether I should go to school to be a minister. It seems I am already there. I know I am more than a massage therapist. I know I am performing exorcisms, and that scares the shit out of me. It's not about being scared of what I do; it's about being scared to tell the world what I do. I have no way of knowing if the battle has been won or if it ever can be. All I know is that these people come to me, and I have to try.

They are sitting in my driveway, walking on the side of the road, and sitting in my living room. I know enough about life to understand that I can plan for pretty beds and fluffy sheets, but that's not what keeps showing up. What comes to me is what is supposed to come. I have faith that what I have been experiencing is what I am supposed to be going through. I must trust that when my dad told me to start writing, he knew this was what would end up on the pages. If you had told me twenty years ago that I would be doing this, I would have laughed in your face.

In June, Conrad and I planned a trip to Rhode Island for our anniversary. We decided to go to Maine to deliver a gift basket of our products to the woman who hosted the essay contest at the Center Lovell. I needed to say goodbye to the white sheets, the basket filled with products, and the secret desire to go head-to-head with Bobby Flay in a kitchen throwdown of lobster bisque.

As we entered the town of Lovell, I couldn't figure out where the town even was. It looked like a series of houses and a few buildings. Despite driving around the lake, we couldn't find a spot that felt like home. We came upon a local restaurant called Ebenezer's that backed onto a golf course. The white lights hanging over the porch reminded me of the dream I had months ago with Metatron when I was on the porch of the Harmon house. As we sat down and ordered our meals, a baby moose appeared on the greens. We went outside with our camera and watched. The moose was sick and dying; its fur looked diseased.

We gave the gift basket to the waitress, hoping its contents would someday reach the woman who gave me back my life. It took many months to come to grips with why it wasn't in my best interest to win that inn in Maine. First, I would have never loved that house or town like I love North Turner. The inn deserved to be loved and cared for, not used as a second-place runner-up. In my mind, I saw it as one step closer to Bear Pond. Second, I would have been too busy taking care of that property to build Foobella's Skincare. I would have never taken the last Reiki Attunements, a significant part of my soaps. My energy products are attuned and blessed, and that would not have ever happened.

The stones only went into the soaps after we visited Lucifer's Falls. Third, there was something more in me that needed to come out. Since not winning, I have learned how to heal myself from lifelong wounds. I am a Massage Therapist, Esthetician, Psychic

Medium, Reiki Master, and the creator of Foobella's Skincare. Conrad is a sound healer, Ordained Minister, and Reiki Healer. I realized that I had my B&B all along. I have cared for my cousins, grandparents, and friends. I have housed homeless people and massaged over a thousand individuals during my career. I have cared for people and helped them cross over. I raised my children, fed the neighbors, and raised money to help others in need. I have done everything I set out to do right where I was.

1 Corinthians is a passage that speaks to me. When I break it down, I understand why it resonates with me so deeply. This is how I see it playing out in my life.

***

Love is patient.

Translation: this is going to take time. Rome was not built in a day.

Love is kind.

Translation: actions that the heart feels are good.

Love does not envy.

Translation: don't want what someone else has.

Love does not boast.

Translation: don't brag to others.

Love does not dishonor others.

Translation: don't complain to people about my partner.

Love is not self-seeking.

Translation: Don't look to justify actions.

Love is not easily angered.

Translation: choose to be happy.

Love keeps no records of wrongs.

Translation: Forgive and let go after you have honored yourself in the process.

Love does not delight in evil.

Translation: Do no harm.

Kathy S. DeMatteis

Love rejoices with truth.

Translation: Tell the truth in a kind and gentle way.

Love always protects.

Translation: guard what is valuable.

Loves always trusts.

Translation: build a foundation based on respect.

Love always hopes.

Translation: Never give up on love.

Love always perseveres.

Translation: If you listen, you will have something special in the end.

We have ruled the jungle and the mighty ships at sea. We have tamed the lions on the Sea of Galilee. We have soaked in the stars high up on the hills and swept through the tunnels into the galaxy of wills. Forever we shall reign; I say it to be so. Let all your woes and worries come crashing low. A mighty lake is calling us with rivers and a gorge, forever, we'll make love and dance upon its shores. I see our future clearly as we thrust upon its wake, dancing in the stars a mighty world to take. The Universe writes all the lyrics; it is the king of all time. Trust in source, oh husband, forever we shall unwind.

***

When I began making all my products, I started experimenting with ways to enhance our lovemaking. Cannabis was one key aspect; it helped me relax and be more open to trying new things. My desire to learn, harness that energy, and incorporate various techniques piqued my curiosity. I experimented with different products and even designed a wrap to help detox the body. Additionally, I created a cannabis muscle blend to use during muscle spasms.

However, I faced significant risks. The products I developed could not only get me arrested but could also result in losing everything I had. Witnessing what the state did to my sister, I felt I had no choice but to discard all my secret products and hide my recipes. Truthfully, I lacked the financial means to bail myself out of jail or help someone else. This was the only way I could proceed. I firmly believe I was put on this earth to help people, especially those struggling with addiction.

Unfortunately, where I currently reside, I have no access to the plant materials needed to create my detox products. I reached out to my legislators, offering to conduct free trials to prove the effectiveness of my creations, but my efforts fell on deaf ears. The pain of detoxing is worse than the flu, and although I have the knowledge, I lack a legal space to practice it.

Therefore, being in Maine was essential for me.

Just as Da Vinci dissected bodies under the Catholic Church's radar, taking great risks to understand how the body functions, others before us have paved the way despite obstacles. Without pioneers like them, we would have been delayed in understanding our biology. Similarly, without my sister Jessica, I would never have learned about cannabis and its healing potential. After all these years, the legality surrounding studying and working with this plant remains unchanged. Consequently, I had to follow in Da Vinci's footsteps—going into hiding to learn what my government refuses to let me do.

The past twenty years as a Massage Therapist, Esthetician, Reiki Master, and Psychic Medium have been the most rewarding of my life. Many of you hold a special place in my heart. We have grown tremendously and delved deeper into ourselves than we ever thought possible. Losing the essay contest for the Center Lovell was the catalyst that set Conrad and me on a journey of healing ourselves and our marriage.

I am uncertain if I will ever see my dream of having "The Center of Love"—a sanctuary where partners grow under the guidance of highly trained healers in the arts of Energy Massage and Body Care. A place to learn how to be in service to one another, opening windows of inner self-expression and transmitting healing messages to your partner through the energy centers. At this point, I wonder if it even matters anymore.

I have thoroughly enjoyed writing and exploring the endless possibilities it offers. Guiding people through meditation has been particularly fulfilling, and I believe my voice is my best tool to move forward. I don't know what the future holds, but I must trust in my experiences. I have faith that when I was led to write my book, it was my true calling all along.

Fast Forward

It has now been six years since I wrote three books and published two of them. What I've learned over these past years is nothing short of miraculous. After publishing my first book, I was cast alongside my husband in a documentary about homelessness directed by Shonta Gibson and Eddie Bell of Let's Go to Work Entertainment. This experience has been one of the most fulfilling moments of my life, making me feel that my work truly mattered.

Upon returning from filming in Las Vegas, I was inspired to write my second book. After publishing that book, I began to experience things I never dreamed possible. In its first draft, I titled my second book, "The Secret Life, The Stimulus Package." It was a compilation of all my hopes and dreams for the future as well as my vision for the world. At the time, I never imagined that I was communicating with people who had passed away, but over the next six years, I discovered that I was. Much of what I wrote has turned out to be true and continues to unfold. People I thought I was inventing turned out to be real individuals I would later meet. The accuracy of their names, physical descriptions, and stories is something I still struggle to comprehend.

Even as recently as last week, I have randomly encountered people who have already been written into my book—individuals I had no idea existed. The precision with which I captured them remains astonishing. During the six years I spent touring the country and promoting my books, there is something I have yet to share. I often wrote with political flair, naming characters after past Presidents. I also discovered that many of the names I used were those of towns in Northern Maine, which I stumbled upon after moving there.

Knowing that my writings have come true leads me to believe that my politically-themed narratives will come to fruition in time as well. Coming out of the psychic closet has been the hardest thing I've ever done—not because it was difficult for me to understand, but because of the many personal attacks on my character. I am criticized for telling the truth. This experience has given me insight into why people lie and why I lied as a child. Only those who pay for the truth genuinely seek it, while the rest of the world prefers to cling to fantasies.

www.ingramcontent.com/pod-product-compliance
Lightning Source LLC
Chambersburg PA
CBHW041308110526
44590CB00028B/4285